MORRIS AUTOMATED INFORMATION NETWORK

0 1029 0586013 0

S0-BBT-977

...SIPPANY BRANCH
449 HALSEY ROAD
PARSIPPANY, NJ 07054
973-887-5150

FEB 2 2 2011

GHOSTS
CENTRAL NEW JERSEY

BIZARRE
STRANGE
& DEADLY

RICHARD J. KIMMEL
Foreword by Marla Brooks

Schiffer Publishing Ltd ®

4880 Lower Valley Road, Atglen, Pennsylvania 19310

Ouija Board is a registered trademark of Parker Brothers.

Other Schiffer Books By Richard J. Kimmel:
World War II Ghosts: Artifacts Can Talk, 978-0-7643-3159-6, $14.99

Other Schiffer Books on Related Subjects:
Cape May Haunts:Elaine's Haunted Manion and Other Eerie Beach Tales, 978-0-7643-2821-3, $14.95
Haunted Bordentown, New Jersey, 978-0-7643-2859-6, $14.95
Middletown: Monmouth County, New Jersey, 978-0-7643-2918-0, $24.99

Copyright © 2010 by Richard J. Kimmel
Unless otherwise noted, all photos copyright of the author.
Library of Congress Control Number: 2009944169

All rights reserved. No part of this work may be reproduced or used in any form or by any means—graphic, electronic, or mechanical, including photocopying or information storage and retrieval systems—without written permission from the publisher.
    The scanning, uploading and distribution of this book or any part thereof via the Internet or via any other means without the permission of the publisher is illegal and punishable by law. Please purchase only authorized editions and do not participate in or encourage the electronic piracy of copyrighted materials.
    "Schiffer," "Schiffer Publishing Ltd. & Design," and the "Design of pen and inkwell" are registered trademarks of Schiffer Publishing Ltd.

Designed by "Sue"
Type set in Eraser/NewBskvll BT

ISBN: 978-0-7643-3442-9
Printed in the United States of America

Schiffer Books are available at special discounts for bulk purchases for sales promotions or premiums. Special editions, including personalized covers, corporate imprints, and excerpts can be created in large quantities for special needs. For more information contact the publisher:

Published by Schiffer Publishing Ltd.
4880 Lower Valley Road
Atglen, PA 19310
Phone: (610) 593-1777; Fax: (610) 593-2002
E-mail: Info@schifferbooks.com

For the largest selection of fine reference books on this and related subjects, please visit our web site at:
www.schifferbooks.com
We are always looking for people to write books on new and related subjects. If you have an idea for a book please contact us at the above address.

This book may be purchased from the publisher.
Include $5.00 for shipping.
Please try your bookstore first.
You may write for a free catalog.

In Europe, Schiffer books are distributed by
Bushwood Books
6 Marksbury Ave.
Kew Gardens
Surrey TW9 4JF England
Phone: 44 (0) 20 8392 8585; Fax: 44 (0) 20 8392 9876
E-mail: info@bushwoodbooks.co.uk
Website: www.bushwoodbooks.co.uk

CONTENTS

DEDICATION

To my many friends and associates within the paranormal community and especially to my daughter Karen, founder of the New Jersey Ghost Organization, for without information provided by their investigative team members much of this book would not have been possible.

FOREWORD

Renowned psychic Marla Brooks. *Courtesy of Marla Brooks.*

New Jersey is known for many things including the boardwalk in Atlantic City, the site of the Hindenburg crash, the Jersey Devil, salt water taffy, Thomas Edison, and of course, "The Sopranos." But did you know that around 180 million years ago, during the Jurassic Period, New Jersey bordered North Africa? Or that around 18,000 years ago, the Ice Age resulted in glaciers that reached New Jersey, and as the glaciers retreated, they left behind not only Lake Passaic, but also many rivers, swamps, and gorges? Or that Native Americans inhabited New Jersey for more than 2,800 years?

In more modern times, the first European settlements in the area were established by the Swedes and Dutch in the early 1600s and New Jersey was one of the thirteen colonies that revolted against British rule in the American Revolution. Another important happening in the Garden State was that the first brewery in America opened in Hoboken in 1642.

Now believe it or not, this very brief history lesson does have a point because in my opinion, where there is history, there are ghosts — and Central New Jersey is rife with haunted locations and tales. From churches to mansions, theaters to cabins in the woods, airfields, and cemeteries, Richard Kimmel knows where to find them and has compiled a fantastic book that even includes a chapter called "A Cauldron of Paranormal Activity," which definitely made me smile.

They say that you can't write about what you haven't experienced so don't for a minute think that this book is comprised of just random and impersonal stories of Central New Jersey hauntings. Many of the locations covered in the book have been investigated by Richard firsthand and, as far as experiencing haunting on a more personal level, he shares his own home with several active spirits.

So if you've ever wondered about which ghosts roam some of Central New Jersey's most famous and historic sights and can't scrape up the airfare right now to visit in person, hunker down into your favorite chair and read all about it. Oh, and when you get to the chapter on the Marlboro Psychiatric Hospital, you might just want to turn on an extra light.

Marla Brooks,
Author and host of "Stirring the Cauldron" on the Para
X and CBS Psychic Radio Networks

INTRODUCTION

Throughout Central New Jersey, the ghostly legends of paranormal activity and intrigue spark the intuitive nature of those interested in putting their sixth sense to the test. For the casual, local, or out-of-town visitor, vacationing at the Monmouth Shore area, with the hope of experiencing a nexus from the other side, is something that they will speak about for years to come — you will not be disappointed.

When walking some of the streets and visiting the historic haunts in Central New Jersey, one cannot help but get the feeling that they are walking in the footsteps of one of America's epic periods in New Jersey's history, the American Revolution. But that's just the beginning. From the famous Matawan shark attacks of 1906 with the victims and heroes resting in Rose Hill, New Jersey's most haunted cemetery, to the legend of Captain Kidd's buried treasure and his connection to Rose Hill, haunting thoughts will creep into your mind.

The intrigue of spies, tragedy, murder, and infidelity haunt the buildings and streets of New Jersey's inland and its coastal towns and, as you continue your journey through these chapters, you will be exposing your mind to the intensity surrounding the paranormal events that reflect Central New Jersey's abundance of ghostly activity. Hearing of the many disembodied voices, images, and noises that have set the eerie scene for exciting experiences…ones that you will not soon be able to forget.

One can only ponder the reason as to why these spirits have chosen to linger for these many years. Seeking answers as to why spirits and ghostly hauntings exist is human nature and one that cannot easily be answered. However, through my experiences in investigating inanimate wartime artifacts, published in my book *World War II Ghosts: Artifacts Can Talk*, the least complicated reasoning

I can offer is that energy remains with or around a specific object or location after the passing of an individual who may have had an affinity to it in life. This energy can be the human spirit itself or energy that has been gathered by the object, embedding itself in some way — or residual energy from an incredibly evil act that has been left behind in its surroundings. Certain rock formations containing quartz or iron ore lend themselves to or have the ability to record the energy from such an occurrence in its immediate vicinity. It is believed that most human spirits will cross over or go into the light after they pass, but because some may have unfinished or unresolved matters in this earthly realm, they remain, seeking to resolve them.

For the better part of the last five years I have been involved in delving into the paranormal nexus and participating in investigations with my daughter's paranormal group, New Jersey Ghost Organization (NJGO). During many of the investigations, I have discovered some spirits to be ambitious, some intellectually challenged, and others intellectually brilliant. There are humorists among them as well as sad ones, pathological liars, good ones, and mean ones. Some fly high and some meander on lower levels while others travel in all directions, evincing curiosity and interest in what we mortals are doing. Spirits can be anywhere at any time. Some ride along with us in cars while others may talk to us audibly through the inner voice, dreams, or by manifesting noises. At times there may be the strong feeling they are trying to help us and at other times they give evidence that they want just to be heard and recognized. There are lonely ones, romantic ones, and occasionally some that would do harm. They come and they go, flitting through our houses at will, sometimes just taking up residence where their fancy directs them.

I have learned also that not only old or historic houses are haunted, but modern ones as well, possibly due to the fact that a modern home may have been built on land that once may have been the site of a prior home from a different time period. A piece of furniture, a bush, boats, or an open field can be home to lingering spirits or ghostly activity. This is especially true for family heirlooms and artifacts that have been excavated from wartime battle sites or wartime souvenirs brought home by servicemen. Most of us have spirit guides that may be a relative, stranger, or just interested entities that use us as protégés for the continuance of their careers on the other side.

Most buildings and dwellings may be host to lingering spirits from time to time; conversely, a house can also be devoid of spirit tenancy. Disoriented, lost, or lonely spirits are more likely to occupy areas that they were most familiar with in life. A sudden death by violence or some earthly tragedy can be responsible for the confusion of the entity that may not realize he or she has passed on. There are also those who are earthbound by choice, seeming to prefer a quasi-life as mortals.

One does not need to seek out a castle in Scotland or England that was built about 500 A.D. to find specters. They are everywhere. You will find them in apartment houses, office buildings, on streets, in the atmosphere, and in churches and cemeteries. I want to stress that they, for the most part, need not be feared, for most are good, friendly spirits. However, we must also realize that where there is good, mean and evil ones may also exist. Demonic spirits can cause harm and attempt possession of body, mind, or home.

Ghosts do not frighten me, but they do enthrall me with their tremendous power and knowledge. I marvel at their mode of travel and how they communicate with one another. Some are clairvoyant while others will attempt to answer questions they are not qualified to talk about. I have learned that to them time is a blend of the past, present, and future, which is difficult for most of us to comprehend.

Recalling my time in the service as an Army combat photographer, thinking back to those days during the Korean Conflict, I can recall seeing certain anomalies in photographs that, at the time, could not be explained technically or photographically. One such anomaly was that of a photograph taken of a six-man patrol unit returning from a mission. This, in itself, would not be uncommon except for the fact that one member had been killed while on the mission and had been left at an aid station upon their return. In the photograph, six figures still appeared, but one of them seemed a bit hazy and not as "in focus" as the other five. Looking back at this, it seems to me that in spirit the fallen comrade was still with his patrol.

You will encounter many spirits that are hazy or unconcerned or forgetful about earthly dates and facts. Occasionally we will run into a spirit that wants to be left alone; others will come poking in to let us know that they are happy. If spirits are pressed for answers to intricate questions, they may balk and show signs of temper and impatience or even cut you off. The talkative ones will chatter along until you stop them or show that you are paying them the attention that they are seeking. At times, it is almost as though they have forgotten their own human frailties of yesteryear.

When it comes to spirits manifesting, we can say from our research that there are many different ways they accomplish this. Spirits can put candles out while others light them, they hide objects or sometimes throw them about, and they may even crawl into bed with humans… as many documented cases have shown. Some have even been known to attempt dragging people out of their beds.

Paranormal investigating or "ghost hunting" can be most exciting because no situation is predictable. Worried homeowners have contacted NJGO, wishing to oust bad ones or to simply find out what is taking place within their residence. However, not all homeowners want to get rid of their ghosts; some are happy in knowing that the unseen residents are that of a relative, while others simply enjoy having them around once they discover that they are friendly. We agree that your spirits or ghosts belong to you and only you should have the right to decide whether to eject them or not. Some people keep pet rocks, and others have pet ghosts.

After reading *Ghosts of Central New Jersey* (and my other book), I believe that you will not simply view them as just other books on the paranormal, but will come away with a better understanding of the paranormal and the technical aspects of researching. I have always felt that any type of investigation should begin with a positive attitude; one of validation as opposed to debunking. Debunking becomes part of the validating process, but should not be the main thrust of an investigation. To those wishing to pursue the paranormal investigation of artifacts, battlefields, and other historic locations, I would offer the following suggestion to be considered when working with the techniques I have here: Above all, remember to always exercise patience. Contacts with the unseen may come when you least expect them.

I have also taken an author's liberty to include with this work several locations in the surrounding areas of Central New Jersey. For myself, these personally have a special significance, as you will understand more fully once you read about them. After my personal experiences, my belief is that they are haunted. As an author, researcher, and investigator, I truly hope that from this work and my previous book that both the paranormal and militia collecting communities will realize that the information gained through research, investigation, and psychic intervention may open new and positive avenues for thought. In the majority of cases, although not considered a science, paranormal investigative techniques and the positive results obtained may change the present historical perspective as we know it to be.

To the skeptic I have just one request: keep an open mind!

My Home's Personal Spirits

In setting the tone for what is to come and what insights are to be revealed in the following chapters, let me begin with my own home. The structure was constructed back in 1940, just prior to the beginning of the Second World War and made entirely of cinder block. This back-to-back, two-family home has not only stood the test of time, but also its welcoming atmosphere…as evidenced in the fact that the spirits of several family members have chosen to remain.

My son-in-law and my youngest daughter now own this family home and live in the rear apartment; my wife and I occupy the front. Two family members have passed away in the house: my son-in-law's great-grandmother and his uncle Walter. The great-grandmother passed away in the bedroom that my wife and I now occupy and uncle Walter passed on in the smaller bedroom that I now use as a den. Another family member, who passed away in an automobile as it pulled out of the driveway, was brought back into the house and kept in the enclosed front porch until the funeral home was able to come and take his body away. These losses have set the scene for what we initially believed to be a residual haunting.

It seems that on many nights, around the same time that the uncle, when living, would come home from work, approximately 12:30, I have seen a shadow figure emerge from the opposite bedroom and move in the direction of the bedroom where the great-grandmother had lay ill for a period of time. The uncle always checked on her after coming home from work.

My son-in-law's brother and his wife once occupied the upstairs level and the uncle would help them out by doing a little cleaning for them. On occasion, when my wife was sitting alone in the living room watching television, usually on nights when my youngest son, who also once occupied the upstairs level, was not home in his room, she could hear footsteps going upstairs. I have been privileged to hear these on several occasions as well, and we are certain that this is also Uncle Walter.

One evening, when I was home alone, I decided to set up my camcorder with night-shot, a DVR, and an EMF meter to see if what I knew from past experiences in the home could be backed up with positive evidence. Beginning around midnight I positioned the tripod with the camcorder facing the hall archway that led from what at one time was Uncle Walter's bedroom (now my workroom) and our bedroom and facing toward the open bathroom door between the two rooms. I dimmed the lights in both rooms to a point where the light was barely visible, while in the bathroom I left the tiny night light on. The lights in the remainder of the home were out and there was no possibility of any outside reflections entering the area. The lights themselves that were left on in the three rooms were not within camera range.

A hamper located just outside and to the right of the bathroom doorway was where I chose to place the DVR and EMF meter, both within camera view. My hope was that Uncle Walter would come home from work at his usual time, which was about 12:30 a.m., and that I would be able to capture his image as he passed through the archway, going into what once was his bedroom.

I did not have long to wait. To my benefit, there was a small reflection coming from the bathroom that had been caused by the infrared beam connected to the night-shot on the camcorder. Uncle Walter came home and presented me with his shadow as he passed the bathroom doorway, temporarily blocking out the light reflection from the commode.

Soon after this experiment, my son Kevin, his then fiancé Diane, and her cousin Stephanie were sitting around the kitchen table one evening. Stephanie has psychic ability and, quite to her surprise, a voice began whispering in her ear. Faintly being able to see the spirit, a young man dressed in a dark tan or khaki uniform began telling her that he is not always here, but that he does come and go. *He* then began to reminisce about the 'good old days'. Stephanie stated that although the spirit appeared as a young man in uniform, he died at a much older age. From Stephanie's experience, we now believe it was Uncle Walter interacting with her, as he did a short stint in the United States Army as a young man, but was released on a medical discharge.

ABOUT NJGO'S PSYCHICS

The experiences set forth in this book are true accounts of contacts with spirits or residual hauntings. All of the investigations were conducted by NJGO and I have personally been privileged to be an intricate part of them, though in most cases the names of the persons involved have been changed or left out to preserve their privacy.

Jane Doherty

When author, psychic, and ghostbuster Jane Doherty lectured at the Breakfast Club, San Francisco's premiere high society club, she turned cautiously minded skeptics into softhearted, warm believers, giddy with their newfound psychic possibilities. Jane is living proof that paranormal abilities can be acquired and, with her first book, *Awakening the Mystic Gift: The Surprising Truth About What It Means to Be Psychic*, she wants to teach that message to the rest of the world.

A renowned psychic for more than fifteen years, Jane has given thousands of readings and is the leading authority on psychic experiences. She provides individual guidance through private consultations, conducts ghost investigations and séances to communicate with the other side, and offers classes and workshops to those who are interested in discovering and developing their own psychic abilities. She was the star of a television series, "Dead Tenants," that is now airing internationally.

Widely recognized and respected for her extraordinary skill and sensitivity, Jane has been featured on Fox Network News, CNN, "The Today Show," "Sightings," "Dead Famous," "MSNBC Investigates," "Jenny Jones," WB11, and in numerous publications, including *The New York Times*, *The New York Post*, *The Industry Standard*, and the *Philadelphia Inquirer*. She was named one of the 'top twenty' psychics by the late Hans Holzer in *Woman's Own* magazine and has been interviewed on more than 150 radio stations including ones in Austria and England. Reuter's news media has featured her in Australia, Austria, Germany, England, Russia, and on the major Spanish network, Telemundo. She also co-hosted a psychic call-in show for eight years and has been featured in three books, as well as in *Woman's World Weekly* and *The Bridal Guide*.

Jane also has the distinction of being retained as an expert government witness for a major U.S. Postal Service mail fraud case involving psychic claims, assisted law authorities in cases of missing persons and homicides, as well as adding to the history of New Jersey when her services were used for an archeological dig. For more than twelve years, Jane was president of the Jersey Society of Parapsychology, which was founded more than thirty years ago for the purpose of providing mainstream scientific research and support to this field. Her ghost investigations have taken her to such notable places as the Lizzie Borden House in Massachusetts, the Palace Hotel in San Francisco, the William Heath Davis House in San Diego, and the Proprietary House in New Jersey, the only original royal governor's mansion still standing in the U.S. today.

Jane says that her most unusual experience was when she was filming her television show "Dead Tenants" and she had to sleep in the same room as a married couple where the couple was experiencing ghostly activity at night. She said that it was odd enough to have to sleep in the same room as the couple, but that she also had to sleep with the cameras on her as they all waited for a ghost to appear. She said that her most amusing experience was when she had to wait for the reported ghosts to appear at a Go-Go bar. She said it was rather distracting as dancers performed onstage and men ogled them from the audience.

Her unconventional job has been quite interesting to say the least, but Jane has a psychic ability that most people do not have. She can be found via her website at www.janedoherty.com.

Lisa Palandrano

When she was still very young, Lisa knew that her grandmother had died before anyone told her. She would get visits in her dreams from people before they passed over. This began when she was twelve-years-old and it seemed that she always, as she put it, "knew things" and thought everyone had the ability to do the same.

Lisa can also see and hear spirits. When Lisa was around eighteen-years-old, she started sitting in with groups of people who had the "gift" so that she could strengthen hers. As a result, her ability has increased tenfold. Lisa has also taken part in many metaphysical classes. She can work with many guides and angels, including the higher spirits of Jesus and Mary. Between her many gifts, she can also offer Shamanic Journey work and is a Reiki Master.

A valuable member of NJGO, Lisa lives in Wanamassa, New Jersey, and can always be counted on to produce positive spirit communication and information gleaned from residual hauntings.

Maryanne Vasnelis

Maryanne is another valued member of NJGO who has had many experiences with hauntings, spirits, and ghosts. She says that as long as she could remember she's had psychic feelings, and in the 1970s she began taking classes in hopes of learning more and to help her explain her feelings and the experiences she had in her early years. Maryanne lives in Edison, New Jersey.

Chapter One:

TAKiNG GHOST HUNTiNG UP A NOTCH

Before we get into the actual hauntings, the following information may be of value in helping you to understand the circumstances and reasoning behind some of the conclusions that NJGO's psychics and I have reached.

Types of Hauntings

There are two common types of hauntings in the paranormal community: one involving the interactive or intelligent haunting, the other residual in nature. One of the misconceptions floating around within the "Ghost Hunting" community is in differentiating between "Spirits" and "Ghosts." A *Spirit* is that of a human being who has passed and can interact with the present. *Ghosts* are images of the passed human or animal that are connected to, what has been commonly termed, a "residual" haunting. A *residual haunting* is the latent energy of an event that has taken place during a previous time period at a specific location and its imprint has in some way been recorded. When the conditions are amicable, it is played back, similar to a "looped" video. The major difference between a spirit and the "ghost" you see in residual hauntings is that you cannot interact with the ghosts. There have been instances during a residual haunting where the voices or sounds of the ghostly participants have been recorded and photographed by paranormal investigators, but that should not be confused with the *energy* that a qualified psychic can detect and receive information from.

Just for your information, there is a third type of haunting and possibly the most frightening — *a demonic or inhuman haunting*. In this case, the entity is similar to a human spirit haunting because it is intelligent and exists in the present moment. Unfortunately, the emotion that is tying them to the earthly realm is usually anger. These entities are malevolent and hostile, suffering from psychological instability or distress that may be from an unresolved conflict with the people who are being subjected to the demonic activity. Demonic presences tend to be "unleashed" in order for them to manifest. This is one reason why the use of an Ouija Board® is customarily discouraged among many paranormal investigators.

Investigative Tips

The first question that beginner "Ghost Hunters" most often ask is: What type of equipment will I need? My response to this question is, "Keep it simple." In fact, you may already possess the basic equipment to begin your quest for the elusive afterlife. One important thing that I must stress is that you should never venture alone on any paranormal investigation for the most obvious reason being, safety. All that you need is a digital voice recorder and digital camera and fully understanding the purpose of these two pieces of equipment and how they operate is essential. The voice recorder will provide the media for a human spirit to interact verbally with you, allowing them to imprint their voice or audible reaction to the electronics within the DVR or on the emulsion of a tape should you prefer using an analog recorder. Working with your digital camera you will be providing a media for a human spirit to imprint their image or to manifest in a form that they are capable of within the electronics of the camera or on the emulsion if you prefer to use a film camera. My belief has always been that if you can see it, you can photograph it.

Interactive human spirits require energy in order to help them manifest and, once detected from the device you are using, will drain its batteries fairly quickly. You should always be prepared for this and have a supply of fresh batteries with you for each piece of equipment being used.

Next, if at all possible, do some research on the location that you wish to investigate. Whether you are planning to investigate an historic location or a private home, ask those who are in charge or the homeowners where they have experienced unusual or unexplained activity. This will enable you to spend your time at the "hot spots" and allow you a better opportunity to capture positive results.

Most important is that you exhibit respect, not just for the surroundings, but also for the spirits that you wish to communicate with. Speak as you would be spoken to and keep your conversation simple; be clear that you're seeking a yes or no, name, number, or color reply. Afterward you should review the evidence gathered as soon as possible and make notations of anything unusual that you may hear or view, even if only for your own records.

One last thought for the beginner ghost hunter would be that if you have psychic sensitivity, this is a definite plus, as it often will take the guesswork out of which spirit or spirits may be present at the location you're investigating. As you become more advanced in your skills, you may wish to join forces with someone who does have psychic ability.

For the more advanced paranormal investigator, what would your reaction be if I told you that all of the above also could be recommended to you? You can enhance your opportunities of the true paranormal experience by returning, so to speak, to the scene of the crime; repeat visits to the same location will allow the active spirits there to become comfortable with your presence and that you mean them no harm. Believe me when I tell you that they will welcome your presence on each of your return visits. I, along with NJGO, have made it a practice that on each return visit to an active location to attempt new experiments…ones that we feel may improve our chances of obtaining positive results. You may even find that certain spirits may work along with you.

One experiment that you may wish to attempt is to introduce negative ions into the atmosphere at the location you are investigating. By doing so, you will create similar conditions to that of thunderstorm activity. This makes what is commonly known as the "veil" thinner and less difficult for spirits to come through. You can, at very little cost, construct a small negative ion generator or you can purchase one. If the location you're investigating has an air purifier and it's not too noisy when running, these are based on negative ions and you can simply let it operate. I may have over-simplified this; however, I wished to present it as less complicated as possible and I would suggest that you do a bit of research in this area, as it may be beneficial for you in the long run.

When venturing to a paranormal conference and hearing individuals from paranormal groups speak or when you're reading various publications, there is no harm in adapting suggestions and certain points that capture your interest into your method of operation. However, keep the thought in mind that a method that may work for one individual or group, may not necessarily work for you.

TV VERSUS PARANORMAL INVESTIGATING

From NJGO Founder Karen Timper

As founder and lead investigator of a paranormal group, I feel it is important that certain aspects of paranormal investigating have some light shed upon it. In recent years, the field of "ghost hunting" — a commonly referred to term, but one that I do not prefer to use — has exploded with television showcasing and presenting paranormal investigating in the entertainment arena. They lend themselves to many inaccuracies and fallacies. Fortunately, most reputable groups are skilled enough to be able to overcome this and garner much more in the way of positive evidence, lending more substance in preserving the future of the paranormal field.

In paranormal investigating, we do use what true science may consider as pseudo-scientific equipment; however, we are not scientists. Therefore, what we accomplish is not recognized in the scientific field as "proof positive" that spirits, "ghosts," or residual hauntings exist. What we do have, with the equipment that we use, is an understanding of basic physics, the laws of thermodynamics, and the theories as to how and why we obtain the results we do.

We are following in the shadows of many great inventors, scientists, and researchers and have modified certain equipment to better suit our requirements. To those individuals, we will forever be indebted. My philosophy and experience in leading a group that has barely scratched the paranormal surface, being in this field for a little over six years, is that the simplest of equipment is all one needs and that knowledge and understanding is a far more important factor. The challenge is in making the equipment work for you — and, once you do, you will find that better results will follow.

Paranormal investigating, via the entertainment media, has created a double-edge sword. Yes, paranormal investigating is exciting and most often rewarding, but because there are dozens of television shows showcasing ghosts and ghost hunting, it has become increasingly popular and there are many more groups cropping up — but for all the wrong reasons. I have noticed that quite a few of the television off-shoot groups seem to fizzle out in a very short time, as they discover that every house is not haunted.

What has become most distressing is that since the "entertainment ghost hunting" shows have come into being, whether good or poorly orchestrated, they have set the scene and many historical locations have succumbed to the "ghost of greed," asking entrance fees to investigate and placing impossible insurance demands on groups. And while time and society have forgotten about many of the historically significant places, many reputable paranormal groups have a genuine respect for history and we do not want to forget about those places.

Yes, the television shows have brought attention to and, undoubtedly, business for these incredible places in history ... but at what price to paranormal investigating?

Chapter Two:

THE GHOSTS OF MONMOUTH BATTLEFIELD

To walk the areas at Monmouth Battlefield at sunset is an experience one shall not soon forget, but do not let your imagination run wild. Rather, focus your mind on what took place here on that fateful day of June 28, 1778. The guns may be silenced now…or are they? Revolutionary War spirits still live on, shadowed by the Continental Army and this historic, tide-turning battle that took place near the village of Monmouth Courthouse (now Freehold, New Jersey), an epic battle beginning at dawn and ending at sunset on the same day.

General George Washington chose this location to attack the British troops that were retreating from Philadelphia to New York City. General Charles Lee launched the assault and, as the battle progressed, without warning or orders from General Washington, General Lee ordered a retreat. The British, under Sir Henry Clinton, immediately counterattacked and only the arrival of Washington and Baron von Steuben prevented an American rout. Steuben re-formed Lee's disordered troops and led them back to battle, but the King's elite forces escaped during the night and the legend of Molly Pitcher grew from this battle.

The historically significant turning point of this major event was General Washington's ride from his headquarters in nearby Englishtown to personally relieve General Lee on the battlefield. Washington's presence on the battlefield, taking command, contributed greatly in rallying the Continental troops and turning the tide of battle with the British, Hessian, and Scottish troops in full withdrawal. Washington's action in relieving General Lee of his command subsequently led to Lee's court-martial: Washington authored the historic court-martial documents at the Village Inn in Englishtown with the actual trial taking place in New Brunswick, New Jersey.

Monmouth Battlefield... Looking toward the area where the house once stood, the house had been used as a field hospital for the Continental wounded.

The Old Tennent Church... Looming eerily as evening begins to set in.

This gravesite of the fallen is shared by the Continental dead. Who they are is known only to God.

This historic battle set the scene for the myriad of paranormal activity there and in the surrounding communities. The brave men on both sides, many of them British, were dying, not from Continental bullets, but from heat exhaustion because of the heavy woolen uniforms they were wearing. Buried locally, a mass grave of Continental troops, whose names are known only to God, is located near the entrance of the magnificent Old Tennent Presbyterian Church and Cemetery in Manalapan, New Jersey, only a few miles from the battlefield and Englishtown.

Having a direct connection with the Battle of Monmouth is the Village Inn located in Englishtown, New Jersey. Circa 1730, this two-story clapboard colonial period structure boasts approximately eleven rooms, an attic, a main staircase, a back spiral staircase, and four fireplaces. Originally a tailor shop, it was sold and expanded to accommodate the new owner's large family. By 1766, it had been

The Village Inn... General Washington used this site as his headquarters during the Battle of Monmouth.

turned into a tavern/inn. Also located on the property are a barn and a cold house where the brew for the patrons was kept, along with other perishable food items.

The Tavern/Inn was a stop on the stagecoach line, creating a busy establishment for not only town businesses, but as a center place during the Revolutionary War and specifically the pivotal Battle of Monmouth. General George Washington, Commander of the Continental Army, resided in a period home only a short walk from the inn, but used the inn as his headquarters during the Battle of Monmouth.

Initially upon arrival, NJGO team members were discussing the Battle of Monmouth and reading pages from a book found near one of the several display cases. During their conversation, the lights in the bar room began to flicker. Usually, when I work with the group, I will do an initial walkthrough, using my pendulum to detect hotspots of latent energy so that my findings can be compared to the psychic's findings.

NJGO'S INVESTIGATION

After our two psychics completed their walkthrough, team members were split into two groups; one team was assigned the first floor, the other the second floor. While on the second floor, one member observed a black figure leaning out from the doorway of the last room on the left side of the hallway, just to the left of the main staircase. Lights would also flicker on the second floor during the team's investigation. Psychic Jane Doherty worked with the second floor team while Psychic Lisa Palandrano worked with the first floor team.

After Lisa and Jane each conducted a separate walkthrough, we were able to have a three-way correlation of the hotspots before the actual first phase of the investigation began. The second stage of this investigation was a séance, which proved to be very valuable to the investigation.

Psychic Impressions

Jane's Experience
During Jane's walkthrough, she experienced a chilling feeling in her stomach — the same feeling she had felt when she was outside

Renowned Psychic Jane Doherty (right) during her initial walkthrough of the Village Inn. On the left is Karen Timper, founder of the New Jersey Ghost Organization, taking notes.

the building and seeing a vision of a hanging of a black man and hearing the names "Frederick" and "Douglass." Once back in the building, Jane's stomach released and the chilling feeling was gone, but near a doorway in the bar area, the lights began to flicker and Jane felt a strong feeling of death…that a stabbing had once taken place in the room just above on the second level. Also felt was a male presence in front of the dining room door.

The reference to the names "Frederick" and "Douglass" is believed to be associated with the American abolitionist Frederick Douglass, one of the most influential lecturers and authors in American history. Douglass himself had escaped slavery. Obviously, the man that Jane sensed being hanged in the Village Inn's yard was not that of Frederick Douglass. What is believed to have occurred was that the spirit was indeed that of a slave during the 1700s and that was the way he made reference to his circumstances…by referencing a powerful figure in history. Perhaps he was one of the homeowner's slaves or was simply hiding at the Inn for fear of being captured by the British. Slaves were hidden during the Revolutionary War out of fear of the British taking them for their own. So even though Douglass came almost a century later, it was just a reference.

Side Note: For some background, here are some interesting facts on Jane's "Paranormal Stomach" as quoted from her website: "Doctors cannot give a medical reason for the bizarre expansion of Jane's stomach as she reacts to spirit energy." What happens is that she can feel spirit energy and somehow it connects to her stomach, becoming sensitized to subtle energy fields. If there is paranormal activity in the area, her stomach reacts.

Walking into the meeting room, Jane feels chills, her stomach is out, and she walks a path in front of both fireplaces, where previously an electromagnetic field (EMF) detector had recorded a reading of five. It now reacted with a reading of eight as she stops between the fireplaces, stating that she feels she is "back in time." She sees images of a meeting that once had taken place and a gavel hitting the table. There are several men...she sees them running out and hiding. Jane's stomach releases after just passing the second fireplace.

As the walkthrough continued, Jane stopped at a window in the small hallway just outside of the kitchenette; her stomach reacted and she felt that there was once a door leading to the outside back of the building where the window now was.

Lisa's Experience

During Lisa's walkthrough, beginning outside the inn, she sensed images of horses with and without carriages coming in and out of the Main Street side of the property near the present gate. She stated that she touched a tree and that it spoke to her, saying that it had been there longer than the house and that many of its brothers had been cut down over time. She didn't sense any spirits at that time, but she sensed people going "in and out."

Inside the meeting room, images began to emerge for Lisa. As it also was used as an eating room, she was seeing images of large tables, but again she felt no presence. In the hallway, Lisa felt that the wood floors were made from the wood of local trees and, as she walked from the hallway into the front dining room and bar area, she turned quickly and uttered the word "ale."

In the kitchenette, Lisa felt that it had been added on at a later time period. As she peered out the window in the hallway, located

An NJGO member accompanies Karen Timper, center, and
Psychic Lisa Palandrano, right, on Lisa's walkthrough.

just outside the kitchenette, she again saw images of horses and
brown chickens. She felt that the Indians had been here first, seeing
images of headdresses.

At this point during the walkthrough, Lisa sensed someone had
died of natural causes upstairs as that area was once a sleeping area,
where as the downstairs was more of a party area. She also had images
of "small bones" and questioned if any baby bones were found on the
grounds. She had the feeling that many people had passed through
here during the inn's longevity and that "important" people had
been here as she was seeing images of men's top coats with the long
style backs. The EMF readings during Lisa's walkthrough remained
at normal levels, indicating that she was receiving psychic images
that were *not* residual hauntings.

The Séance

Later, Jane conducted a séance after the major part of the
investigation wound down. One of the goals of the séance was to
see if there was additional evidence that could be captured with our
equipment and if specific spirits could be pinpointed.

As the séance got underway, the general feeling, almost immediately, was that there were spirits — *at least two* — coming through to both Jane and one other team member. The feeling was described as a pressure emanating from above their heads and down to their shoulders. An overwhelming feeling of sadness began to overcome some of the team members, bringing uncontrollable tears to their eyes. One member, feeling the head pressure, also felt a bleeding or seeping sensation as though their head was wrapped in some sort of bandage. It also felt webby, similar to a feeling of a fine spiderweb on their skin.

At times during the séance, lights flickered and everyone heard the sound of quick, short, light footsteps from the main staircase on the second floor and what seemed to be a knocking emanating from the far corner of the meeting room.

Members' Experiences

† One member felt a heavy breathing sensation and saw his father's face; his father had passed on when he was only six months old. He also felt pressure on his lap as though someone was sitting on it.

† Another member experienced the most traumatic sensations: freezing cold, sadness, and pain in the back. As the pain became more intense, the member may have blacked out for a few seconds because the next thing she recalled was her face being wet and that she was actually crying.

† In more than one instance, team members sitting next to an individual having an experience *also felt the experience* through the connection of holding hands. The experiences seemed to have been mimicking what had taken place in this location, as during the Battle of Monmouth both soldiers and civilians stayed nearby or at the Inn.

Is the War Over?

Spirit interaction seems to pop up when you least expect it. During the séance, two interactive spirits of soldiers from the Continental Army were encountered, seemingly in hiding and not aware of their demise. Jane told them that the war was over and that they no longer needed to be hiding. One of them asked Jane who had won the war; the Continental Army was her reply. Their reaction seemed to be that of peace…their duty here on this earth plane was now complete, so Jane proceeded to help them into the light and to cross over.

I cannot imagine a more fitting end to this investigation. It's hard to explain the feeling one receives, knowing that you were able to help those lingering gain peace and to move on.

Chapter Three:

IS THE DOCTOR IN?

CENTER HALL

Circa 1830, this Center Hall Colonial home is located in a small town in the vicinity of Freehold, New Jersey. Between 1927 and 1929, two different physicians occupied the home. Frequently footsteps are heard in the hallway outside the master bedroom late at night and there have been times when visitors have reported hearing a woman's voice humming or singing coming from the shower area in one of the bathrooms. Several guests have reported seeing the image of a lady dressed in a flowing blue dress standing at the landing of the huge main staircase leading to the second level of the home.

Legend of the Lake

Located just across the road from the house is Weamaconk Lake, host to the eerie legend of the 'Lady In White', believed to be the spirit of a young woman who had taken her life because of her husband's infidelity. Not many facts can be recalled about the mysterious "Lady of the Lake," but for a few. One resident, a very young girl at the time, recalled hearing of the incident being spoken about when visitors came to her home. Not being permitted in the room, she nevertheless was able to hear bits and pieces of what the adults were discussing.

It seems that the young lady in question had been concerned about rumors she was hearing that her husband was seeing another woman. Upon following him one evening, she was shocked to find the rumor to be true. Distraught by what she had witnessed, instead of returning home she simply walked into the lake… presumably ending her problem, but did she? From time to time residents claim to have seen the apparition of a young woman in a white dress standing on the far side of the lake. It seems that she may still be wandering around, seeking a resolution to the unfinished business of her husband's infidelity.

Weamaconk Lake... Home to the "Lady in White."

NJGO'S INVESTIGATION

The current homeowner called in NJGO to hopefully validate the reported sounds and sightings being experienced.

Located on the far edge of the property, the foundation is all that remains of the gristmill that was once located here and which served the neighboring communities. Originally built in 1778, it was consumed by a blazing inferno of unknown origin in 1922. The site poses an eerie presence on foggy days with the wooded area and winding stream that continues its path behind the property...you get a feeling that more has been left behind than simply the foundation. To those with a keen sense of smell, the lingering odor of smoke has been detected on the anniversary date of the fire.

At times, on the opposite bank of the stream, beavers can be seen felling the slimmer trees, dragging the logs to the stream's bank, and floating them downstream to build their dams. Presently, the only activity at the site of the old mill is its current use as a patio by the present owner. The home still houses the original large floor safe and a Bunsen burner that was in use during its occupation by the two physicians.

Paranormal Phenomenon

The following phenomena have been reported:

† Smells of smoke occurs during the month of September in the early afternoon.
† Upstairs, near the main staircase, the floor creaks frequently.
† The image of a woman in a blue dress is seen on the main staircase, and humming/singing can be heard from the "Blue" bathroom on the second floor.
† Members observed an item being thrown from a built-in corner cabinet.
† A discarnate voice has been heard at times.
† One guest in the home claims to have played with a young child on the second floor.
† During one of NJGO's investigations of the home, which is a continuing situation as the group has their monthly meetings there, I, along with team members and the homeowner, have experienced hearing something hit one of the glass shelves of a metal frame decorative shelf unit. All were present in the same room and, when attempted, the sound could not be recreated. The sound was also picked up by one of the quad video cameras that were on at the time.

The Spirits

Several spirits occupy this home on a regular basis. There are also *visiting spirits* — ones from the Revolutionary War era that occasionally stop by, as the home was a stopover during the war.
The spirits include:

† A female spirit dating from 1932 and whose name begins with the letter "M" (Marie or Marion).

† A male spirit that is tied to the land or house; the name/word "justice" was received…perhaps he was a slave or former employee.

† A little boy is believed to have lived here at some point in time. The boy, who came from a well-to-do family, has blond hair and is wearing knickers, a nice shirt, and bow tie.

Summary

Although there were no significant changes in temperatures, there is definitely a great deal of energy in this home that can be associated with paranormal activity. No source was discovered that would account for the electromagnetic field readings. The evidence captured substantiated a majority of the phenomenon reported by the homeowner. NJGO's investigation here is an ongoing process.

Chapter Four:

THE SPY HOUSE

PORT MONMOUTH'S HAUNTED REVOLUTIONARY TREASURE

Located in Leonardo, New Jersey, on what was once a lightly traveled road, is what has become known as the infamous Spy House, set back between the road and a stretch of beach. The first section was built in 1648, with two additions constructed at later dates. Prior to it being temporarily closed for renovation, it was — *and still is* — host to, at the very least, twenty plus spirits. Not all of its past inhabitants are present at one time, but you can be certain to run into a few, in various forums, at each visit. So come prepared.

The legendary "Spy House."

This house was a tavern during Washington's day and got its name because the owner would put the welcome mat out to British troops, listen to what they were planning, and then pass the information onto Washington's men (hence the name Spy house). This was before it was used by pirates who supposedly hid treasure near the house and stored their dead in the basement. There are tunnels under the house and there have been ghosts seen of both a pirate and a child who died in the upstairs. Soldiers were murdered there also. So with all this history, the Spy House has been described as the "Grand Central Station of Ghosts" in New Jersey.

The Spirits

† A visitor was looking for her child and saw a woman in period clothing hanging draperies. When the visitor spoke to the woman, there was no reply, which would lead one to believe that this may have been a residual haunting.

† Near the fireplace in the main room were two captains' chairs and, when the spirit of a sea captain is present, the chair he is sitting on has a definite change in temperature from that of the other…feeling extremely cold to the touch. I personally experienced this temperature phenomenon on a visit many years ago.

† Another story claims that a father and son were standing near the parking lot at the rear of the house, facing the water. Now, it is not uncommon to see individuals fishing at the far side of the parking lot, but as the father and son stood there watching, they noticed one of the fishermen walking towards them, seemingly going to his car. As the fisherman walked along, he began to *pass through* several of the cars, as if he was walking a path that no longer existed. As it got closer, the apparition became more visibly transparent and then disappeared completely.

† A bit more bazaar is the story of a 'nasty' sea captain who occasionally sits in the back, windowed room of the second floor. Running almost the entire length of the house, the room

faces the water and New York City, which was a stronghold of the British Army during the Revolutionary War. On occasion, he is known to bother visitors.

† There is also the voice of a child, believed to be a young boy, coming from the top of what once was a staircase, but has since been encased in the wall.

Many other spirits come and go at various times, so when you visit the Spy House you never know who or what will make its presence known. The downstairs fireplace in the main room seems to be a portal that the spirits make good use of on their journey between realms.

One of the most intriguing accounts to come forth is that of a young lady walking down the front path from the house as a horse-drawn carriage pulls up in front. The young lady gets into the carriage and, as it begins its journey down the street, it seems to disappear into thin air.

It would be a true experience to spend the night in the house; I most certainly would like to, as I am certain that most of you would too.

A closer view of the pathway where, on occasion, witnesses have sighted the spirit of a young girl going to meet a horse-drawn carriage.

NJGO'S INVESTIGATION

It was just after the sun had begun to set when NJGO's team of paranormal investigators approached the Spy House. They immediately experienced the ominous feeling that they were being watched, a common sensation that most people feel when daring to visit here after hours and the building is closed. I should preface what I just said with the main reason that the group was there that particular evening: it was their annual function that they call "Dining With The Ghosts." This may seem to some as being unusual, as most often the affair is held at an outdoor location, complete with candelabra and, hopefully, one or two spirits. At the rear of the building is a small picnic area with benches and tables and, after eating, they decided that since the building was closed they would simply walk around and take a few photographs of the outside and possibly through some of the windows.

As luck would have it, one of the county park rangers, since the building is under their jurisdiction, happened to come by to lower the flag for the evening. When the group explained what they were doing there, he was kind enough to let them in for a short while. Right now the Spy House is closed to the public due to restoration that is taking place and was void of any furniture. Unfortunately, very little was captured that evening except for the lingering feeling that they were under constant surveillance by past — *unseen* — residents who still resonate in this jewel of American history.

Chapter Five:

SPIRITS OF THE PROPRIETARY HOUSE

The ghosts that haunt the Proprietary House in Perth Amboy, New Jersey, are alive and well. The house, which was built in 1762, is the only standing home of a Royal Governor in New Jersey. William Franklin, son of Benjamin Franklin, was New Jersey's last Royal Governor from 1762 to 1777. At the time of his appointment, there was no official governor's residence in the state.

In the 1680s, early settlers to the then-colony of New Jersey staked out the land around what was then called Amboy because of its convenience to New York, including the waterways that surrounded it. When William Franklin was appointed Governor, he chose this town to be his home and the newly built "House of the Proprietors" was the house he chose. William Franklin only lived in the home for two short years before his shameful arrest and imprisonment for his alleged behavior as a traitor.

In the nearly two and a half centuries since the Proprietary House was the home of William Franklin, it has served many purposes. At one time it was an orphanage, a home for disabled Protestant ministers and their wives, as well as orphans of deceased ministers. It was also used as a private residence on many occasions and was a seaside resort for a period of years. It has also been a hotel and a boarding house until its ownership was transferred to the state of New Jersey. The Proprietary House Association, which is an historical society, now runs it and the house is listed on the National Register of Historic Places.

As a result of the many inhabitants who have lived here, as well as the many British troops that surrounded it during the Revolutionary War, this house is filled with ghostly activity. On ghost tours, renowned psychic and ghost hunter Jane Doherty explains what occurs when a ghost is present. According to Jane, a ghost can present itself in many different forms, such as through a vision,

The Proprietary House stands in all its eeriness. *Courtesy of NJGO.*

an odor, or a cold spot. This is a result of the ghost's attachment to a person, place, or thing in their lifetime.

Well, it seems there are many people who were attached to the Proprietary House. There have been reports of a soldier dressed in Revolutionary War attire who walks through a wall. Upon further research of the location, it was found that this is the exact spot where a tunnel existed that was used by troops during the Revolutionary War. There have also been many reports of a woman standing in the window of a second floor dining room. One report was from a police officer who patrols the area and asked that the caretakers of the house

"remove the mannequin" from the upstairs window. He was informed that there are no mannequins in the house. Neighbors have collaborated the policeman's report, saying that they too have seen a woman standing in the window.

In addition to these two spirits/ghosts, there have been many other reports of ghostly sightings both in and around the house. Several reports of a "little boy in blue" who is quite oddly dressed is said to have, on one occasion, let a deliveryman into the house, leading him upstairs to an office on the third floor via an elevator. Unbeknownst to the deliveryman, no little boys live in this house...*at least not now.*

The spirit of the little boy is that of Jonathan and he met a tragic and untimely end at the hands of his uncle when he was pushed from a third floor window. History has not provided many details about the circumstances that surrounded this tragic event. However, in one of the second floor rooms, the boy likes to play with a ball and a tiny male doll when he is not roaming in the building.

According to Jane, when she walks into an area of a building where there is ghost energy, her stomach expands. This odd occurrence was proven during a recent ghost tour: a male volunteer from the group confirmed that Jane's stomach did in fact expand and then contract when she walked away from the alleged "ghost spot." Jane says she senses a lot of ghost activity in this house; in the center of the upstairs drawing room, she gets the feeling that a heated argument between two men had once taken place, followed by one of the men throwing a pile of papers at the other and storming out. Historic belief is that during a visit to his son's home in 1777, Benjamin Franklin and his son William had a serious argument, and the elder Franklin stormed out of the room after throwing papers at his son.

Examples such as this are aplenty, as Jane experienced similar feelings in many rooms of this house. She has seen a soldier walk

This séance at the Proprietary House was done prior to NJGO's investigation. Note the orb that appeared near the head of one of the members sitting at the extreme right.

through the walls and has had the vision of a room full of beds lined up. Later reports confirmed that the house was once an orphanage and that several children shared a bedroom. There have also been sightings of a little girl standing in the corner of the gift shop on the second floor.

On the night of a recent tour, a guide was waiting for his next group to begin their tour on the second floor. As he waited, he heard a loud stomping up the stairs. He ran upstairs thinking that someone had attempted to bypass the line for the tour, only to see a pair of legs from the knees down in tan pants and tan shoes. He said, "I've been coming to this house for forty years, and that's the first time I have personally seen anything, but I saw it!" The next night at the same time, the same man was in the same spot and heard the same stomping up the stairs, but did not see anything at that time. However, Jane says that it is not unusual for ghosts to have a "pattern" in which they will appear at the same time on different days.

NJGO'S INVESTIGATION

NJGO recently conducted a thorough investigation at the Proprietary House, capturing startling evidence that confirmed what visitors and those who oversee this historic landmark have experienced over the years.

With Maryanne Vasnelis, one of NJGO's psychics, present that evening, before beginning the actual investigation, we decided to hold a séance, just to warm things up a bit and to let the spirits in the building get to know us a little. Two members of the Proprietary House staff were present and confirmed some of the information that Maryanne was able to garner.

At various times during the séance, contact was made with the little boy, Jonathan, who periodically asked Maryanne for the little red and white ball. Maryanne knew nothing of a red and white ball — at least not until the end of the evening. When we were breaking down the equipment, NJGO founder Karen Timper came across a tiny red and white ball that she always brought on investigations. The purpose of the ball was for experimenting…to see if an entity would move it while we videotaped the experiment. The ball was at the bottom of Karen's equipment case, which had been closed all evening, so we were puzzled as to just how the spirit of Jonathan knew that it was there....

Summary

While the group was busy collecting their equipment, I still had a couple of pictures left on my digital camera, so I decided to go up to the main floor. The lights were still out when I arrived, but by the light of my flashlight I was able to make out a beautiful period mirror hanging on the wall immediately to the front of me as I entered the doorway on the right side of the room. There was also a doorway on the same wall to my far left. I snapped a photograph of the mirror and then another one. I then returned to where the rest of the group had gathered, waiting for me.

When I return home from an investigation, no matter what time it is, I have always made it a practice to load my photographs into my

This famous "mirror photo" was taken during the investigation at the Proprietary House, revealing two interested spirits. The three inset have been enhanced for better viewing.

computer. However, it was not until the next morning that I actually viewed them. When I came upon the one of the mirror, I could not see any reflections, as it was completely black so I decided to lighten it. The old saying is "What you see is what you get," but in this case it was "What you *don't* see is what you get" — I had captured two distinct images being reflected in the mirror from the doorway that was to my left, appearing to have been watching. The image on the right appears to be that of a gentleman in colonial garb, complete with cutaway coat and tri-corner hat; the other is of a woman in period dress. This proves the point that spirits will embed their images, appearing when least expected, and are as interested and curious in what we mortals are doing as we are of them.

Chapter Six:

SPIRITS AT ROSE HILL CEMETERY

Located in Matawan, New Jersey, Rose Hill Cemetery has been cited as the most haunted cemetery in New Jersey. Dating back to pre-Revolutionary times, Rose Hill has been host to the infamous pirate Captain William Kidd and his legendary lost treasure. At the highest point in the cemetery, Kidd is said to have selected one of three tall pine trees, still standing, to use as one of his guideposts from the sea. The other guidepost was a tall pine tree, no longer standing, that was located near the entrance to the Navasink River. Somewhere between them, it's believed that Kidd buried his treasure...

Facing the front entrance to Rose Hill Cemetery as NJGO members arrive for their evening investigation.

NJGO Founder Karen Timper, left, along with several members, view what may be the legendary "tall pine tree" located at the highest point in Rose Hill Cemetery — the one that "Captain Kidd" may have used as one of his guide points to his buried treasure.

The most likely spot of the buried treasure would be in the area of Cliffwood Beach. The pirate supposedly moored on the Raritan Bay before his capture and subsequent trial. Legend held that Kidd buried his treasure on Money Island, which was located just off the coast of Cliffwood Beach at the mouth of Whale's Creek. Eroded by treasure hunting excavations and shifting sands, the island disappeared sometime during the 1900s.

The best time to arrive at Rose Hill is just prior to sunset, so that you can experience the full impact of what may await you. Definitely one should not venture here by themselves. Set into a hillside are several old mausoleums, most in need of some repair. When you walk to the top of the hillside, you will find yourself at the highest point in the cemetery. This is the location of several high pine trees; on windy nights, you can hear the sound of whistling and the trees bending to the rhythm of it. A strange, light-headed feeling may overcome you, along with a feeling of despair… The thought crosses your mind that it may be time to leave....

Shark!

The victims and the heroes of the Matawan River shark attacks of 1916 are buried in Rose Hill Cemetery. Beginning as most summer days had in the past, July 12, 1916 was no exception, barring the fact that by day's end two people were dead. The unexpected shark attack took place along the Matawan Creek.

Since temperatures were nearing ninety degrees, Captain Thomas Cottrell decided to close his little bait and tackle shop. While trying to cool off a bit from the heat, Cottrell was standing on a drawbridge that spanned the creek when he suddenly noticed something black hasten by in the water below. Realizing what it was, the thought crossed his mind as to what a shark would be doing in the creek this far from the ocean.

Twelve-year-old Lester Stillwell and a few of his friends were upstream a short distance preparing to go swimming. Only a short time had passed when one of Lester's friends, Charles Van Brunt, noticed a large black fish flash by him and heading right toward Lester. The boys could see the shark's gleaming white teeth and underside as he attacked Lester. The boys shuttered at the screams of Lester as he was being dragged beneath the surface. Unable to help him, they exited the water as quickly as possible and went seeking help. It was not until two days later that the body of Lester Stillwell surfaced about 250 yards upstream from where the shark had attacked him. The young boy's body had been horribly disfigured.

Watson Stanley Fisher was part of the rescue team. In the meantime, Captain Cottrell had somehow been able to commandeer a motorboat and began to direct the rescue effort. During this heroic rescue effort, the shark attacked again; this time it was Fisher who received the thrust of the shark's venom. Somehow managing to break himself loose, he miraculously made it out of the water. After a tourniquet was applied to his wound, a local doctor, Dr. Reynolds, was sent for and he was transported to the Matawan Railway Station to be taken by train to Memorial Hospital in Long Branch. Severely wounded on his lower extremities from his groin to his kneecap, flesh missing from his right leg, finally around 7:30 p.m. he succumbed to loss of blood as he was being taken into the operating room.

Now, the time had arrived for the folk in Matawan to bury the dead, and Rose Hill Cemetery was chosen as the place to be their final resting place. Throughout the horrid incident, Captain Cottrell was deemed the hero of the day and, eventually, he too found his last resting place at Rose Hill.

NJGO'S INVESTIGATION

When we first arrived at Rose Hill, parking our cars near the pond area, little did we know what awaited the group as evening drew near. Our arrival was just prior to sunset and the area was beginning to take on an eerie appearance. It was almost as if it was an invitation into another realm. We decided to begin our investigation with a walking tour, so that when darkness set in we would be better prepared as to where to venture during the evening's investigation.

As the dark of night began to fall, you could hear the croaking of frogs coming from the lily pad covered pond. The winding roads added to the mystique of the evening. The main road leading into the cemetery at the point of the pond makes a loop, circling around the hill, and returning to the pond area. We divided into several teams, but then the unexpected happened. Our psychic Lisa announced that several of Rose Hill's residents were on the hill located across from the pond, sitting among the headstones, observing us. They seemed to be very interested in what we were doing.

Our quest that evening was to make contact with the victims and heroes of the famous Matawan River shark attacks. Oddly enough, the grave of one of the victims was located in the exact area of the hillside where our spirit observers were — that's where one team had begun their investigation. Fortunately, we were able to locate the gravesites of Lester Stillwell and Captain Cottrell; however, despite several other visits to Rose Hill, the gravesite of Watson Stanley Fisher still remains a mystery.

The gravesite of Lester Stillwell... He was one of the victims of the infamous shark attack of 1916.

Summary

Walking Rose Hill at sunset, when darkness begins to set in, you will have the feeling of stillness in the air, broken only by the occasional croaking of a frog. You can see the lights from several homes dotting the perimeter of the cemetery. If you're using a voice recorder in hopes of capturing EVPs (Electronic Voice Phenomena), especially during a summer's evening when people are sitting out in their yards, occasionally stray voices will be recorded as sound travels at night. Once in a while, a stray night animal might cross your path, harmless but scary. NJGO has been fairly successful on each of their visits to Rose Hill. On occasion, we have met others there who have made successful contacts with Rose Hill's inhabitants, and you may too…just be prepared for the unusual paranormal experience.

Chapter Seven:

HAUNTINGS AT THE PRISON MUSEUM

THE IRONY AND THE GOVERNOR

One of the most haunted places in America — Burlington County Prison Museum — is located on the fringe of Central New Jersey in Mount Holly, New Jersey. Considered to have an abundance of paranormal activity, its history ranges from murder to the infamous New Jersey Governor Hoffmann, and Albert DeSalvo, who was later to become known as the Boston Strangler.

Description

Burlington City, founded in 1677, was the first settlement in Burlington County, the capital of the Province of West Jersey and the county seat until 1796. The first jail was located in the basement of the courthouse. This was replaced in 1767 by a separate stone structure that was used until 1811 when the Burlington County Prison in Mount Holly was completed and ready for use. When the county seat was moved to Mount Holly in 1796, the federal-style courthouse was built in the same year. It took another fifteen years, however, to purchase land for the prison site and have plans drawn up and approved by the freeholders. The purchase price of the land was $2,000 in 1807 and, when finally completed, the new prison's construction cost a grand total of $24,201.13.

The outside of the building has changed very little. The massive front door, the large hinges, and the lock are original. The interior vaulted ceilings of poured concrete and the brick and stone construction are also much as it was when the facility first opened. The interior is whitewashed, as it would have been when first occupied. The cell doors are also original and many were fabricated in place.

This eerie view of the Burlington County Prison Museum was taken from the warden's house. *Courtesy of Karen Timper.*

As formidable as the prison seems, it was not escape-proof. The walls were scaled and the roof penetrated numerous times in its history. The preferred routes to freedom seem to have been through the roof of the jail and the passageway to the warden's house next door. One notable escape occurred in 1875. A hole was punched through the ceiling of an upper corridor cell to gain access to the roof and the escape of four men was made good by climbing down a woodpile next to the prison yard wall. A fifth accomplice, too large to fit through the hole and incensed at being left behind,

reportedly sounded the alarm. Despite a quick response by the warden, it seems that at least some of the escapees were never caught.

Many criminals were destined to spend their last days on earth in the Burlington County Jail. State law mandated that criminals convicted of a capital crime were to be executed in the County in which they were found guilty and Burlington County was no exception. Numerous public hangings were conducted in the prison yard on gallows erected for each occasion. The last such execution was the double hanging of Rufus Johnson and George Small. The two men were convicted of murdering Florence Allinson of Moorestown, an English-born governess at a refuge for homeless children. Solved within days by the celebrated Burlington County detective Ellis H. Parker, the men were hanged March 24, 1906, two months after the crime.

Solidly built, this prison was in constant use until November 1965. Originally designed to house approximately

Front view of main prison entrance. *Courtesy of Karen Timper.*

An inside view of one of the prisoner's cells.

forty prisoners, the Burlington County Prison held over one hundred inmates when they were moved to a converted armory that formerly stood behind the jail. Overcrowded conditions required yet another larger prison, which was erected in 1983.

Prison Life

When the prison was originally designed, each "guest" of Burlington County was to have his own cell with a fireplace and a narrow window placed above eye level. The rules of the jail directed that prisoners were to be bathed, deloused, and have their clothing fumigated and that each cell should have a bible or prayer book "to improve the soul." Individual cells, intended for felons or criminals,

These reconstructed gallows are located in the prison yard... Several inmates met their demise on them.

were arranged in sets of four, opening off of a short hall at each end of the building. These "blocks" of cells were to house separate groups, such as habitual criminals, first offenders, and women. The larger rooms on the main hallways were to accommodate the debtors, imprisoned for owing money. These were common rooms, sometimes holding three or four men at a time. During the day, debtors were allowed to move about the jail, performing various cleaning chores or employed in the basement workshop.

The "dungeon," or maximum-security cell, was in the center of the top floor. That location was carefully chosen to prevent escape by digging, minimize communication with criminals in the cell blocks, and ensure constant surveillance by guards making rounds. This was the only cell without a fireplace. It is flanked by niches for guards or visitors and has one very high, very small window and an iron ring in the center of the floor to which the prisoner could be chained. As one might expect, tradition states that this cell is haunted. Supposedly, the ghost of Joel Clough, a murderer who spent his last night there, has paid tribute to his last earthly residence and to the vigilance of the prison guards in later years.

Originally, two rooms on the main floor were set aside as the living quarters for the "Keeper" and his wife. The Keeper's wife was expected to supervise the female inmates and the Keeper was to execute the "Rules of the Jail" as devised by the Prison Board, which was comprised of members of the freeholders. The Keeper and his family lived in these quarters until the adjacent brick house, connected by a passageway, was constructed on the corner of Grant and High streets.

In keeping with the intent designed into the structure, the basement level contained a workshop where prisoners were expected to learn some useful trade, such as how to make brooms, baskets, or shingles. Another, less supervised, pastime of the inmates that endured through the ages was prisoner graffiti. Depicting humor, despair, and a belated piety, several fine examples of this art have been preserved through photographs and are on display throughout the building. The felons' eating room, also in the basement, permitted controlled access to the exercise yard with its twenty-foot wall. Outside, prisoners could tend to a small garden of fresh vegetables. In one corner of the yard there was a set of leg stocks to punish unruly inmates, and an area was set aside for the gallows, which were dismantled and stored between hangings.

Staple foods, linens, cleaning supplies, and craft materials were stored in the basement near the kitchen, baking, and washing facilities. Once a day the prisoners were to be served a main meal of meat and vegetables. The other two meals were usually cooked cereals or grains. They had milk and cider to drink, as well as water. Until 1928, the prisoners prepared their own meals. One of the inmates was made chief cook and slept in a basement cell next to the kitchen. Large washtubs provided for laundry and regular baths for the prisoners.

NJGO'S INVESTIGATION

NJGO has conducted several investigations at the prison, resulting in startling evidence being captured. Psychic Jane Doherty accompanied NJGO on a recent visit to the prison and was able to confirm the paranormal activity that museum supervisor Marisa Bozaarth and other museum personnel had felt was taking place there. Though Jane went into this investigation not being told anything about the haunted activity in the prison, she was able to have come forth to her information that had not been previously known. While NJGO members set up their equipment, Jane did a walkthrough on each of the three floors. Karen Timper, the group's founder, accompanied her, taking notes of what Jane was experiencing.

Psychic Impressions

Jane's walkthrough began on the front porch of the prison and her curiosity is first drawn to three houses that were directly across from the prison. She sees horses and carriages lined up facing north on High Street; a sense of importance, some sort of procession. *(This can be interpreted as a funeral procession for perhaps a prisoner or the sense of importance may have meant something related to New Jersey state representatives on official business.)*

In the gift shop, located on the first floor, Jane's initial impression is that a famous victim from the county — a murderer — had once been incarcerated here. *(This was determined to have been Richard Bruno Hauptmann of the famous Lindbergh murder case).* Also visualized is a historic figure from the 1860s *(Civil War years)*, someone from the Princeton, New Jersey, area, which is approximately thirty to forty minutes from the prison. *(Prison staff validated this impression as being the county's famous first Detective Ellis Parker, who worked on the Lindbergh case.)* Then-Governor Hoffman asked Parker to take the Lindbergh case. Bruno Hauptmann, the man sentenced for murdering the Lindbergh baby, was incarcerated at this prison, but the Governor did not want to be embarrassed, nor the newly formed New Jersey

State Police to be potentially embarrassed, so the true murderer's identity was suppressed. *(Captured on camera was a fast moving orb in the Warden's Office.)* On a previous NJGO visit to the prison, the staff had reported that the smell of pipe smoke has often been experienced. Jane believes that Parker's spirit still lingers here in the prison. She sees him on this floor, smoking a pipe and looking through papers.

The next stop on Jane's walkthrough was the second floor. Her initial impression as she ascended the wooden staircase, entering the north wing, was that it was "spooky." She did not like this area at all, as she visualized a "shift guard" standing at the end of the wing. Jane's *psychic stomach* began to react just before reaching the door of a cell that she said she wanted to enter. As no one is normally permitted to go into this cell, Ms. Bozarth unlocked it for Jane, whose stomach was still reacting strongly. As Jane walked half way into the cell, she began experiencing strong spirit energy of a hanging or suicide and a guard finding the victim. *(The prison staff validated this impression as they indicated that there had been a few suicides in this cell.)*

As Jane moved on, passing the window of another cell, her stomach again reacted and she began to involuntary move in a rocking motion while standing there. She said that she did not feel comfortable doing it and does not know why she is. Feeling that there was a great deal of writing done in this cell, she sees coins, stamps, drawings, and doodling on paper. Since this was a maximum-security cell, Jane suggested that the walls might have absorbed a lot of the prisoners' energy. Furthermore, because this was a one-person cell, Jane felt that some good electronic voice phenomena might be captured and suggested that an NJGO team member remain here and conduct an EVP session.

Moving along down the wing, Jane came upon two separate cells that had been opened to make one large room. The second cell door had been cemented shut and she saw this room as being used as a church or for a church group to gather. She felt that there was no bad energy here and she received the names "Violet" or "Viola" *(possibly making reference to a musical instrument)*. Ms. Bozarth recalled that at one time she had brought her violin into the prison, as she wanted to try playing it there because the acoustics were good in this cell. No one ever new or was told of this until now.

The south wing's energy is not as strong as the opposite north wing's. In what once was a bathroom or tub area, Jane saw a lot of shenanigans and planning that went on. She felt an escape or scuffle, the breaking down of a door, and perhaps even a death had happened there. Her stomach began to react while standing on the platform covering where the tub once stood beneath a narrow window. Continuing with her vision, she sees a stabbing, possibly with a razor, and blood. She also hears a man's voice cursing and senses a lot of anger. She hears more than one voice. All of this began escalating into a much larger event. *(The prison staff validated this impression, as they indicated that five inmates had attempted to escape through the window; four were able to get out and were subsequently captured later, but a fifth one did not make it through the narrow window because of his body size).* On previous NJGO visits to the prison, some team members experienced the sensation *(vertigo)* of moving/motion sickness in and on the tub platform area, which other members had witnessed.

In the main hallway connecting the north and south wings, a fast moving, high density orb, resembling a baseball being thrown, was captured on video. The origin of the orb appeared to be coming out of a photograph on the wall of the only two prisoners who had been hanged at the prison.

Entering the basement from the southern end, Jane felt extremely uncomfortable at the foot of the staircase. A feeling of isolation came over her and she is repelled, her stomach reacting strongly in front of the cell where an inmate, Harry Asay, resided. Harry was responsible for the brutal murder of a guard and another prisoner and was subsequently sent to an insane asylum in Trenton, New Jersey. There he had undergone treatment and was released. There was an eighteen-year gap between that time and when he was again returned to the prison. This time it was for being drunk and disorderly. However, when he was first incarcerated here, it was for the theft of tires and it was his goal when he arrived to kill a guard. He accomplished this by delivering a blunt force trauma — a single blow to the guard's head — using an iron poker from the fireplace that was located in the kitchen/cook's cell as the murder weapon.

On a previous NJGO visit to the prison, members were able to capture positive audio and video simultaneously in the area of the

This inside view was taken in the basement facing the area where the guard was bludgeoned to death by prisoner Harry Asay... it shows the staircase where the body had been dragged.

stairs, where the bodies of the slain guard and inmate had been dragged to and placed under. No staff or NJGO team members were present and the voice recorder had been placed in a stationary position at the stairs location, as was the video camera that had been placed facing the stairs. A sinister laugh, believed to be that of Harry Asay, is heard, quite possibly after he murdered the guard or maybe the laugh was produced to intimidate or was a sign of triumph in his accomplishing his goal. The video produced an anomalous, self-luminous "squiggling" object moving rather fast across the screen in a horizontal position. This is believed to have been the energy of Asay.

In the workshop area, Jane sees two men mulling around. One man is of color, the other Caucasian. Jane was overcome with the feeling that a prisoner that was allowed to work in this workshop

Left to right, NJGO Founder Karen Timper stands by the door of what once was Harry Asay's cell, where Jane is experiencing extremely strong paranormal energy.

should not have been trusted. She feels that the Caucasian inmate did not feel comfortable and did not want to work with the one of color. She visualizes this as being sometime back in the 1800s or at least not in "modern times," meaning the 1900s or Millennium (2000s). She sees the Caucasian bolting from the workshop. During one of NJGO's previous visit to the prison, another one of their psychics *saw* someone running down the hall in the same direction as that which Jane saw. And this psychic also saw a large man of color in the workshop who went by the name of "John."

Jane was receiving the names "Ray," "William," "Williams," and "Willie." From the wing that was just opposite to the workshop, where the guard was murdered, Jane's stomach began to react and she reports seeing an active spirit that lurks or walks this area. She feels that it could be the guard that was murdered. Following the "path" of the energy, Jane continued down the hall, past the kitchen/cook's cell, and follows it as it turns left into another wing. Her stomach returned to normal as she stopped before a cell that is now a men's bathroom. The previous psychic was mentally and physically startled upon walking up to that same door and opening it, as a bright flash of "red" light greeted her.

Could this have been the last stroll of the guard before he was murdered? He may have entered the hallway from the stairs at the end where the men's room is, checking the end cell first as he left the wing and continued down the hallway toward the kitchen/cook's cell. Just before the workshop doorway, he was attacked. Harry Asay's cell was just around the corner in the wing adjacent to the workshop's second door that was across from his cell. Asay is believed to have hid in the workshop, jumping out as the guard passed, striking the single blow to his head. It is unclear if Asay actually murdered the inmate that was in the workshop at the time, but he also had killed another inmate besides the guard. Why Jane's stomach begins and stops reacting on the "path" is because it's either an active human spirit or a residual haunting that keeps playing over and over of the guard recalling this route he had walked — his last walk and last thing that he remembered before he was murdered. *(The prison staff confirmed that this guard was in fact that of a former warden Harry King, who at times doubled as a guard in the prison.)*

As the walkthrough returns to the main (first) floor, Jane's initial impression is of seeing a lot of bananas being peeled in the gift shop area. Fruit would have been cheap and possibly in abundance to feed the prisoners. *(The prison staff's interpretation of Jane's reaction was that the prison in recent months had put in a request to the county or town of Mount Holly to display a paper mache "monkey" as part of an art exhibit.)* As Jane walked through the warden's office, she stated that she felt fine with the energy in there and continued on toward the women's wing.

Upon entering the wing, straight ahead of Jane, coming from the cell at the far end, she hears a woman screaming, being beaten and raped by a male guard. The male guard taunts and teases, resulting in death, of a naked female. Jane feels that prisoners were at times displayed outside for humiliation, a fact that the prison staff confirms. Jane receives the names "Paul," "Hall," "Sarah," and later she gets the name "Diana."

NJGO set up a video camera in that same area after Jane's walkthrough had concluded and turned out the lights. On review, they found that three distinctive orbs had been captured on tape, moving quickly from the cell straight ahead. At one point, you can clearly here a distinct click as the camera shuts off and again when it's turned back on. The turning on and off of the video camera by itself showed no time loss on the display; however, the date reflected a completely different one — not the default date, but one that was eight days in the future from the date that we were there. Was there *someone* that did not want us to see the "rape" and perhaps the three guards who were involved that caused this lapse in the date, yet with no lapse in time? Your conclusion is as good as ours. Later, during a séance that Jane conducted before we concluded the evening's investigation, she felt that this particular female *(referring to the rape victim)* had given birth in the cell and that the prison staff had tossed the baby outside into the prison yard, but that the baby had first been smothered.

The warden's living quarters are connected to the prison by an enclosed walkway that overlooks the "gallows" in the prison yard. There are three windows and, even though Jane reports feeling very low energy there, as she peers into the prison yard she sees many people standing in line. At this point, Jane becomes very tired and decides that she will walk around the prison yard on another visit. Later, during the investigation, several orbs were captured in the bridge area and near the small area between floors a photo of a dark, lurking figure was captured.

Summary

With a team of investigators on each of the three floors, it was lights out! The investigation commenced with Jane doing a second tour on each of the floors, but this time with each of the investigating groups. With video cameras rolling, still cameras clicking, and voice recorders in hand, the teams' hope of capturing spirit activity was not disappointed. Spirits in the prison seemed anxious to be heard in one way or another, embedding their voiceprints on the recorders and making the K-2 EMF detectors flash as they responded to questions being asked. With their images being visualized on video and still media, one could not help but to feel confident in the investigative procedures that evening.

At approximately 11 p.m. Jane and the investigating teams returned to one of the second floor cells to conduct a séance. All of those present that evening took part in the séance, sitting in a circle, and clasping each other's hand. Jane felt that having the large iron barred door to the cell closed during the séance would make for a more realistic atmosphere and that any spirits present may react in a more positive way. Jane immediately sees "the guard" standing directly in front of her. We noticed that one of our video cameras shut off with a lot of time remaining on the battery. There was a feeling of coldness in the air and everyone's feet felt extremely cold. The guard's cold breeze was felt, with some members feeling a touch on their cheeks and others on their arms. Another investigator's video camera's battery was completely drained. Jane experienced a hanging and was informed by the spirit of a prisoner that he did not do it. *(Prison staff confirmed that a prisoner had been framed and that it was the uncle of the victim and someone else that committed the crime.)*

Voice recorders were placed on the floor at various positions, as were EMF detectors. A video camera was positioned and two members of the investigation team were poised, one to take still photographs and the second to record the slightest sound or voice using a sonic microphone connected to earphones and a digital voice recorder. Other than the detection of a couple of spirit residents of the prison and that one of the team members became nauseous during the session, nothing out of the ordinary presented itself.

At one point Jane saw "the murdered guard" standing behind her during the séance with his arms crossed. He was anxious to know what the purpose was of us being here. Some things were spoken about during the séance, and Jane mentioned that there are more bodies buried in the prison yard than had previously been known by the staff. *(The staff is currently aware of bodies buried on the south side of the yard closest to the building.)*

Another significant psychic discovery, added to what had already been known and confirmed, was that of a cold-blooded murder on November 5, 1920. For this to fall into perspective, I must relay this in two parts. Keep these two November dates in mind: November 5, 1920 and November 1, 2008. On November 1, 2008, when NJGO participated in the prison museum's annual Halloween haunted house activities, a ghostly skull-like image was captured on a still camera. This full-bodied apparition had no feet and appeared to be floating or hovering.

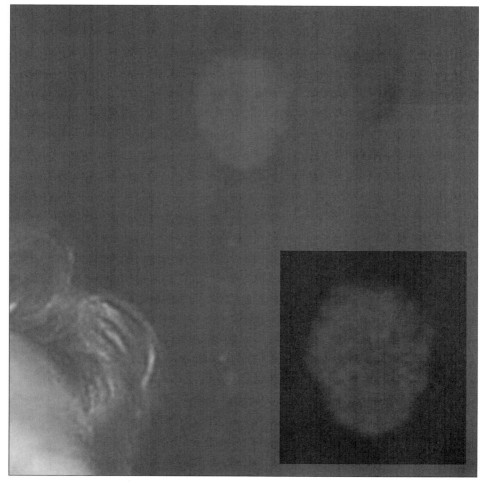

Rare and unusual is this first time capture of an anomaly outside the prison on the lawn. Psychic Jane Doherty believes it's the spirit of Harry Asay.
Courtesy of NJGO member Richard Wisenfelder.

Psychic impressions of this photo indicate that something looms over the prison as a result of two entities at odds and ready to do battle. *(The second entity was behind the photographer.)* One entity is, or was, an inmate at the prison who was killed. The psychic's make-up of this skull-like entity fits the physical description of Harry Asay, who murdered Warden Harry King by blunt force trauma and also attacked prisoner Charles Bartlett on November 5, 1920, which coincided as a possible anniversary date, almost to the day eighty-eight years later.

The ironic connection that NJGO has with the prison is that the group's first meeting place was at the museum in a converted church in the Historic Old Bridge section of East Brunswick *(see Chapter Ten)*. Housed as a permanent exhibit in the museum is the elephant collection of former New Jersey Governor Hoffmann, along with his personal papers. His parents are buried at Chestnut Hill Cemetery, just up the road from the museum *(see Chapter Ten)*. Former Governor Hoffmann was very active in the famous Lindbergh kidnapping trial that had taken place back in the early 1930s.

Chapter Eight:

MIRACLE IN MONROE TOWNSHIP

For those who may not now be believers in spirituality, spirits, and ghosts, you may become a believer after a visit to this shop. Large yet quaint, this religious shop is located in Monroe Township and deals in spiritual items, offers a prayer room for patrons who wish to meditate, and an area on the second level for those who wish to peruse the many books that are available. Most of the items in the shop have been either completely handcrafted, or at least partly, by the owner.

The shop owner, at left, shows NJGO members photographs that were taken on various occasions in the shop.

During the years, many regular patrons have had many religiously connected experiences within the shop, as well as visions and dreams. Photographs of hundreds of anomalies in connection with the events have been taken, leaving little to explain. After all, a photograph is worth a thousand words...

A visit my daughter Karen and I made to this shop turned out to be a very special day, as the glove of Padre Pio and bone fragments of Saint Teresa of Ávila were being brought there to be on display. Both of their presences were felt.

St. Pio of Pietrelcina (May 25, 1887-September 23, 1968)

A Capuchin priest from Italy who is venerated as a saint in the Roman Catholic Church, he was born Francesco Forgione and given the name Pio when he joined the Capuchins. He was popularly known as Padre Pio after his ordination to the priesthood. He became famous for his stigmata.

On September 20, 1918, while hearing confessions, Padre Pio is said to have had his first occurrence of stigmata; bodily marks, pain, and bleeding in locations corresponding to the crucifixion wounds of Jesus Christ. This phenomenon continued for fifty years until the end of his life. The blood flowing from the stigmata is said to have smelled of perfume or flowers, a phenomenon mentioned in stories of the lives of several saints and often referred to as the *odour of sanctity*.

Painting of Saint Pio.

View of Saint Pio's glove.

St. Pio's stigmata is regarded by some as evidence of holiness and was studied by physicians whose independence from the Church is not known. The observations reportedly could not be explained and the wounds never infected. It was reputed however that his condition caused him great embarrassment and most photographs show him with red mittens with brown or black coverings on some. Over the years, scandal with allegations of stigmata fraud have been attempted, even though observers saw the disappearance of the marks from his hands and feet where the bleedings occurred. Believers deem this as yet another miracle.

The incorrupt body of Saint Pio of Petrelcina was exhumed from his crypt March 3, 2008, forty years after his death, so that his remains could be prepared for display. A church statement described the body as being in "fair condition"; only the top part of the skull was partly skeletal, but the chin is perfect and the rest of the body was well preserved and that the stigmata are not visible. St. Pio's hands "looked like they had just undergone a manicure."

It was hoped that morticians would be able to restore the face so that it would be recognizable. However, due to its deterioration, his face was covered with a life-like silicone mask.

Cardinal Jose Saraiva Martins, perfect for the Congregation for the Causes of the Saints, celebrated Mass for 15,000 devotees on April 24, 2008 at the Shrine of Holy Mary of Grace, San Giovanni Rotondo, before the body went on display in a crystal, marble, and silver sepulcher in the crypt of the monastery. Padre Pio is wearing his brown Capuchin habit with a white silk stole embroidered with crystals and gold thread and his hands hold a large wooden cross — 800,000 pilgrims worldwide, mostly from Italy, made reservations to view the body up to December 2008, but only 7,200 people a day were able to file past the crystal coffin. Officials extended the display through September 2009.

At Padre Pio's death in 1968, his body appeared unwounded, with no sign of scarring. There was even a report that doctors who examined his body found it empty of all blood.

Summary

NJGO members and psychic Jane Doherty were present the day that Saint Pio's glove was on display. At one point, Jane positioned herself in the corner of the room where the glove was displayed to see what would come through to her and had received the distinct impression of the presence of Saint Teresa.

After returning home from this day's experience — touching the glove of Saint Pio and being able to see close-up the bone fragments of Saint Teresa — I had no thoughts as to the surprise that would await me upon viewing the photographs I had taken. Seeing what appeared at first glance to be a common orb in one of the photographs, I decided to enlarge the image area. What I discovered was *not* the common orb that I expected to see, but rather a very unusual star or sunburst anomaly containing the distinct image of a cross! I am certain that in some way this anomaly is connected to the items that were on display and possibly even having a greater significance.

Left to right: NJGO member Lori Steiner, NJGO founder Karen Timper, (anonymous gentleman who brought the bones of Saint Theresa in for viewing), and psychic Jane Doherty discuss the day's conclusions. Note the "starburst or sunburst" anomaly near Karen's head.

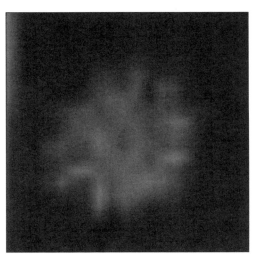

Unusual starburst or sunburst anomaly containing a cross that made its presence known.

Chapter Nine:

GHOSTS LOVE TO READ

RARITAN PUBLIC LIBRARY

Considered the most haunted library in the state, Raritan Public Library — the former General John Frelinghuysen House — is located in Raritan Township in Central New Jersey. Dating back to the early eighteenth century, this historic house was partially restored as a library in the early 1970s.

Visitors have come away with stories that the old library keeper haunts the library nightly, turning on lights and moving books. There have also been numerous sightings of the elderly woman in one of the windows and in the old garden behind the library. People who live near the library have seen the lights go on and off at very odd hours. They claim that the old woman died there. Even psychic and ghost hunter Jane Doherty sensed the presence of several specters during a visit to the library.

BERNARDSVILLE PUBLIC LIBRARY

The *haunted* Bernardsville Public Library has a strange history of sightings, as well as a very mysterious and historical past. The library is located on Morristown Road in Bernardsville and was constructed in 1710 as the Vealtown Tavern. Captain John Parker, with the help of his daughter Phyllis, owned and ran the tavern. During the Revolutionary War, the tavern became a common place for the army to stop for a stay or just to rest. There have been numerous ghostly sightings reported at Bernardsville Public Library:

† In 1974, after some renovations were done to the library, employees started to claim that they had seen Phyllis' apparition. One employee even saw an apparition of a man dressed in eighteenth century clothing peering through one of windows.

† In 1987, a group of people held a séance; today library patrons in the local history room can view a videotape of this séance.

† In November 1989, while in the reading room, a young child saw the ghost of a woman wearing a long white dress. He told his mother that he said 'hi' to her, but that she did not answer him back.

Other occurrences that have been reported from time to time include hearing muffled conversation throughout the first floor, footsteps on the staircase, and the rustling of a skirt. It seems that objects move around on their own in the kitchen area, and there have been numerous sightings by patrons, librarians, and police officers of a female figure in Revolutionary style clothing logged. Oftentimes, someone looking inside the building afterhours will sight the apparition from the outside of the building.

Many ghost hunters have searched and tested the Bernardsville Public Library for paranormal activity; most have claimed to encounter a disturbance, but some disagree on whether the disturbance comes from the spirit of Phyllis or that of some other spirit.

Chapter Ten:

HAUNTED EAST BRUNSWICK

THE HISTORIC DISTRICT OF OLD BRIDGE

Tucked away in the southern part of East Brunswick is the Historic District of Old Bridge. South River borders it on two sides, on the east and south; Chestnut Hill Cemetery, on the north; and Route 18 and Old Bridge Turnpike, on the west. Due to its favorable geographical location on the navigable part of the South River, the area attracted settlers as early as 1685. It derives its name from the fact that the first bridge spanning South River was built there and, as other bridges were built across the river, the first one became known as "the Old Bridge." Prior to that, it was known as South River Bridge. Although the village had never been chartered or incorporated, it nonetheless grew. Through its long history, the village had numerous names, but none were as meaningful or as permanent as Old Bridge. The Historic District of Old Bridge is on the New Jersey State Register (September 1975) and on the National Register (June 1977). It is the first township in Middlesex County to have received this distinction.

One gets a strange feeling while walking the streets here in the Historic District. The homes, some dating back to pre-Revolutionary times and the Civil War period, present a feeling that one is walking back in time. Known by very few, except for the residents living there, some of these magnificent relics of the past are haunted.

The historic and haunted Appleby-DeVoe Memorial Library...

Guardian of the Broach

The first library in East Brunswick was established on what is now Main Street in the Historic District. Known as the Appleby-DeVoe Memorial Library now, it stands as a true monument to the early settlers of the township. Herbert Appleby was a Civil War veteran who served in two New York regiments. Upon his return after the war, he married Mary Foss in 1866 and their daughter Alice was born in 1868. Abbie, their second daughter, passed away at an early age in 1880. A third daughter, Laura V., was born in 1881. Alice, Herbert's wife, passed away in a sanatorium in 1917, where she was hospitalized after being severely injured in an automobile accident. Herbert died inside the house in March 1921.

In the fall of 1984, Richard Walling, son of the late Mayor Jean Walling of East Brunswick, went to the building to review some of Mayor Walling's files that were kept in storage in the former library. Seeing the caretaker's car missing, Walling decided to ring the bell anyway, thinking that perhaps the person might be at home. Standing at the side door, he rang the buzzer and could hear it sound in the kitchen immediately above the doorway. He rang it once and then again, until he heard a woman's voice call out from the kitchen window, "I'll be right there!" Walling stepped to the side of the house and called up to the window, "Okay!" A minute passed...and then another... Walling looked around and realized no one was home. Humming quietly to himself, he went back to his car and left. To be sure about what had happened, he called the caretaker the next day and she told him that, indeed, she had not been at home, nor was anyone else there.

Who had called out to him that afternoon? Was it Alice or Abbie Foss? Was it another person who had formerly lived in the house? Maybe one day we'll know, but for now, all we can say is that there is at least one permanent resident of the old Appleby house on Main Street.

For a brief period NJGO was fortunate to have been able to use this location as a meeting place early on in their formation, affording them the opportunity to experience and document, firsthand, the paranormal occurrences there.

My own personal experience here actually goes back several years during one of our meetings. While the group's psychic Lisa Palandrano was working with me, examining several of my artifacts, I happened to pick up a broach that was laying on a table near where we were working. No sooner than I had, the former owner of it came through to Lisa, very concerned that someone may take the

"Guardian of the broach"... This dress was worn by Alice Appleby, whose spirit now stands guard over her broach (inset).

broach. A chill ran through my entire body and I quickly placed it back on the table. Lisa assured the spirit of the former owner that her prized possession was secure and safe. From that point on, the spirit worked with us during our longevity at the house.

A Historic Cemetery

Just up the hill from the Appleby-DeVoe Memorial Library, you will find the beautiful Chestnut Hill Cemetery, home of some unusual and historic gravesites. A stroll here is like reliving the past of the Historic Village of Old Bridge. You will see the resting places of families that were so vital and important to the development of the Village.

When you walk to the center of the cemetery, you will enjoy a panoramic view of the Village and it will seems like you can see

This unusual gravesite is believed to be that of American Indians. Note the mosaic insets and designs that were placed on the headstones.

forever. As you gaze at this vast territory, you realize that this was once home of the Lenape Indians. The obelisk in the center of the Rogers' plot (at the center, top of the cemetery) is a memorial to William A. Rogers, a young resident killed during the Civil War. The weather has taken its toll, as it is now impossible to read the inscriptions.

Looking downhill from the top of the cemetery (facing toward the Historic Village), you will see the Grand Army of the Republic (GAR) Memorial plot; here many of our men who served in the Civil War are buried. About one hundred yards to the east, you will see the stone marking the resting place of a former slave, Curliss Boles.

When President Lincoln freed him from slavery, Mr. Boles did not wish to leave the family he had once served. The Squires family brought this man from the South to Old Bridge and put Mr. Boles to work in their hotel and ice business. In his later years, Mr. Boles was afflicted with an incurable disease and John Squires moved him to a small building on Pearsal Road, close to the pond where Mr. Boles' remaining days were spent. When Mr. Boles passed away, John Squires buried him with dignity and placed a granite marker on his grave.

In 1983, several graves were discovered along River Road in East Brunswick. The burials belonged to African-American slaves that worked for the Barkelew family in the late 1700s. The burials were disinterred and moved to Chestnut Hill Cemetery.

NIKE MISSILE BASE

Fire in the Hole

Located at the end of Old Jake Brown Road in Old Bridge, adjacent to East Brunswick, is an abandoned NIKE missile base. Access to the former base can be gained from Route 9 just before or after Route 516, depending which way you are traveling. Very few individuals are aware of why the base and its surrounding homes were deserted so quickly and only the roads that once led to the houses are still in existence.

This is the first view one sees when entering the old NIKE missile site.

Site of the barrack and headquarter buildings... Vacated by the military, they are now occupied, partially, for use by the state.

When first entering from the highway, easily seen is a rusting round metal structure with a silo-type roof and a metal staircase leading up to its door that is believed to have once been part of the water supply for the base. As you continue in, you will see several gray metal structures that once housed storage, workshops, and possibly the headquarters for the base. Next, you will come upon a deserted baseball field with only the backstop still standing. Just beyond this is the field area where a group of small one-family houses once sat; they were abandoned shortly after the base closed. The structures most likely served as homes for some of the employees of the base. At the far end of this little community is a locked gate leading to the old missile base that was dedicated in the early 1970s. The State of New Jersey now owns the base.

When my daughter Karen, founder of NJGO, and I ventured to the site one day around sunset, we had the distinct feeling of not being wanted. The atmosphere suddenly became still, so we decided to hightail it out of there…possibly even more quickly than did its previous inhabitants.

It is rumored that the site is haunted and that there is a constant mist within the area no matter the time of day. The lingering question, among many, in our mind was, why did the former residents leave in such a hurry? This has yet to be answered; however, back in February 2008 authorities were called to investigate after bones were discovered there. The details are a little sketchy as to what exactly was found at the site and it is unknown whether the nature of the find was of animal or of human origin.

A now lonely view looking toward the entrance to the area where the missile silos were located.

"HAUNTED" LODGE ON THE LAKE

Elk's Lodge BPOE 2370, located in East Brunswick, is the second most haunted building in the township. The original structure was built in the early twentieth century as the private estate of the owner of Nixon Nitration Works, which included a number of plants and covered about twelve square miles on the Raritan River, near New Brunswick, in what was then officially known as Raritan Township and unofficially as Nixon, New Jersey. Lewis Nixon, naval architect and industrialist, created it in 1915 and, upon the outbreak of World War I, was geared to supply some of the warring nations of Europe with gunpowder and other materials.

This view of the "haunted hallway" was taken from the Gold Room. A shadow figure has been seen several times by members when closing the lodge for the night.

Built adjacent to the main house was a smaller house, where Lewis Nixon resided most of the time as he used the main building for his library and for entertaining. During the days of Prohibition, a tunnel leading from the lake into the basement of the building was used to bring in booze. It was also a passage for ladies of the night on various occasions. Today covering most of the tunnel is the foundation of an addition to the lodge; however, under this foundation one can still have access to a portion of the tunnel area, which resembles an eerie miniature catacomb. When this addition was constructed, it also covered a beautiful Italian marble patio that is still underground and cannot be seen today.

The lodge is only open to Elk members and their guests; however, do not let this deter you from visiting. Part of the grounds is open space and you can park your vehicle and view the lodge from the outside. If you get there around sunset, the surroundings and the stillness of the lake may just set the scene for some unexpected paranormal activity.

NJGO'S INVESTIGATION

Since I am a member of the lodge, I made arrangements for my daughter's group, NJGO, to conduct an investigation to hopefully confirm or lay to rest the many experiences that members claim to have experienced over the years. In Elkdom, the tolling of Eleven Strokes is significant to Elks around the world, as everyone stops in remembrance of the brothers who have passed on, never to return again…*or do they?* What we do know is that the lodge is believed to be haunted, so do some members return? NJGO and I were about to find out.

The atmosphere surrounding the lodge lends itself to spirit activity from the property's early history, hosting a nearby Revolutionary War skirmish to possibly an early gravesite being discovered in a clearing between two towering pine trees and the apparition of a little girl seen sitting on the smaller building's back steps that is now used as the home for the lodge's caretaker. This caretaker has reported having several unusual experiences in the main building during her time here.

Inside the lodge is a different matter. Several of the lodge members have experienced visions of a shadow figure moving from what is known as the Gold Room into the narrow hallway and passing through the wall into what is now a restroom. It is interesting to note that originally the restrooms did not exist, as this area was used then as a ballroom. Also, when locking up the lodge for the evening and turning off the inside lights, the light in the Gold Room will turn on again by itself. Members have also reported being touched, hearing unexplained noises and voices, and having just plain, eerie feelings.

During the investigation, we encountered several spirits, including a Revolutionary War soldier named Henry; a woman who once worked at the lodge named Mary; and the spirit of a cat. Needless to say, we were not disappointed. As we made our way to the lower level of the lodge to the area known as the "catacombs" — passages cut into the earth that were original to the building before it became a lodge — we were surprised to find that the spirit of Mary was with us. Our spirit host explained that one of the passageways once led to the rear of the lodge, where "booze" during the years of Prohibition was smuggled into the building from the lake; her terminology made us chuckle. However, what we did not expect came next, as Mary enlightened us to another use of the underground passageway: the original owner would use it to bring, unobserved, ladies of the night into the building. This had always been rumored and now our spirit host was substantiating that.

The investigation culminated with a candlelight séance in the Gold Room by NJGO psychic Lisa Palandrano. Another psychic, Maryanne Vasnellis, was also present. Positioning two video cameras with night vision capability at opposite corners of the room, we had complete coverage of the séance table from two different perspectives.

As the séance progressed, one of NJGO's new members was asking a series of questions of the Revolutionary War soldier spirit Henry. At one point, Henry either became tired of the line of questioning or may not have liked the direction it was taking and decided to put an abrupt end to it — *he* sent an energy charge that two members who were sitting opposite of the questioner felt. As the energy charge passed through them, one member was zapped with such a force that it made him jerk back into his chair and stand up. Henry must have used a considerable amount of his energy to accomplish this transfer, as we could not make contact with him for the remainder of the séance.

Chapter Eleven:
TULIPWOOD'S GHOSTLY TREASURE

The parcel of land that was to become the property currently known as Tulipwood is located at 1165 Hamilton Street in Somerset and was part of a 121-acre tract owned by Mary Maclay Williams since 1877. This sprawling estate adopted its name from the many tulip trees adorning the property, only a few of which are still standing. The home was built for Stephen Guion Williamson in 1892 and was the third house built by the Williams family at the interconnecting site along Hamilton Street.

Under one of the still standing tulip trees lays the ashes of one of the home's former owners and their presence is still strongly felt in the home, watching over the estate. However, it is not the only entity that lingers at Tulipwood. The structure itself is home to several spirits and a piece of furniture with an attached mirror is a portal to the other realm. On many of NJGO's investigations here, several images have been seen and photographed in this mirror.

Tulipwood...as it stands today.

Psychic Lisa Palandrano has seen residual images of American Indians roaming the land adjacent to the home. Psychic impressions from within the various rooms have yielded extraordinary occurrences, including one that took place two days after the last investigation, at another location, related to a retired Gift Shop Manager who, at the time, was working as a museum office manager and docent at Tulipwood.

Once you enter the foyer of this magnificent home you will almost immediately be taken back in time. Yet a feeling of strangeness overtakes you when you marvel at the large paneled fireplace and mantle on the left and the bookcases that are built into the wall on the right. Facing you is the magnificent paneled staircase leading to the second floor. The first landing of the staircase immediately arouses your sixth sense... *Did something traumatic once happen there?*

Tulipwood's magnificent mantel can be seen in the foyer as you first enter. Orb enthusiasts will immediately take note of the energy orb appearing near the mantel.

Equally intriguing is the room immediately to the right with its own fireplace, large windows, period fixtures, and two corner cabinets. Empty now, this once was the dining room, from which you can enter the butler's pantry. The kitchen areas present itself in the magnificence of its period — you can almost smell the food being brought in by the servants and hear the dinner conversation of the former occupants. In the kitchen, you will find the servants' staircase winding its way to the second floor and opening into an

One of Tulipwood's elegant rooms just to the right of the foyer that was used as the main dining room. Note the orb located near the chest at the front of the photograph.

area opposite and separate from the residents' sleeping quarters. At times a presence can be felt emerging from this staircase... Could it be that of the butler or another servant?

In one of the rooms, temporarily used for storage, was located a dresser with a mirror and, as most paranormal researchers know, mirrors can be a portal in which spirits easily access the present realm. Now, I never pass up the opportunity to photograph mirrors when on an investigation and this was no exception. When viewing

This mirror is believed to be a portal for Tulipwood's past residents. In the inset close-up, you can see their images.

the accompanying photograph, disregard the center deterioration of the mirror's silvering and look *into* the mirror, not at it. There are several images that appear… One of the more significant seems to be that of a young lad wearing knickers; he is believed to be the original owner as he appeared in his youthful days. I was later shown a photograph of the owner standing with a group of other children that had been taken at another location in which he was wearing knickers. If you study the photograph, you will see other former residents of this realm…*how many you can find?* It seems that former inhabitants of the home were as curious as NJGO and I were during this investigation.

NJGO'S INVESTIGATION

Psychic Impressions

On NJGO's first visit to Tulipwood, Lisa, one of our psychics, felt a strong male presence attached to the house and saw a male entity moving from the butler's pantry and kitchen area up the back staircase to the second floor bedroom area. Also detected was a "newborn baby" smell in the front bedroom on the second floor and an unknown presence lingering in one of the far corners of the attic.

Psychic Lisa Palandrano, on first going into the home, felt extremely cold and immediately sensed "fire" associated with the house as she entered the foyer. She stated, "I feel that some kind of fire had gone a little out of control…enough to cause black smoke in the foyer."

Lisa added that when she was walking the grounds before entering the building, her visions were taking her far back in time. She was sensing Native American Indians all around, particularly one young Indian man about twenty years of age standing very close to her. She stated, "Outside I sense Native American Indians hunting. I feel that they knew of water not far from here, a small creek." Perhaps this was sensed behind Tulipwood's main structure. Lisa also said, "Fighting…Indians fighting."

Lisa also had a vision of men hanging from trees beyond the front lawn, across Hamilton Street, where there were now houses, but back then there were just trees. She also had a vision of owls associated with the property where Tulipwood sits, as well as other animals, including horses, elk, and moose, from a period long before the house was built. The strongest energy that Lisa felt was that of the spirit of the young Indian man. She stated, "He defended this land and lived on it with his family."

Later in the afternoon, Lisa stated that word was coming through to her of a large hole or tunnel and questioned if the land had been used during wartime. She added, "I can see soldiers underground, sneaking through."

What is extremely important to this investigation is something that Lisa also noticed, beside the smell of smoke, on first entering the home. When she stood near the woman — the retired gift shop manager — and looked at her profile, she noticed that she could not see the woman's aura or soul. Lisa mentioned this to Karen, the investigation's leader, shortly before the conclusion of the investigation.

Independently, one of our other psychics on the investigation, while seated in a corner of the main room in the dining area, heard a man's voice whisper in her ear, "I wonder how the old woman feels knowing she is going to die soon." Who this spirit was and why he said this to our psychic remains a mystery, but his words do not... Two days after our investigation the woman in question perished when her home, only a few blocks from Tulipwood, mysteriously burned to the ground. Would it have changed the outcome if she had known the message that our psychic had received? You must judge this for yourself...for if you believe that the Lord's will is to be done, then nothing would have altered this situation.

Summary

As a fitting close, should you visit Tulipwood, you will not want to miss seeing the lone, waxed tulip flower that is sitting in a shaped glass on the main mantel in the foyer. This was taken from one of the large tulip trees still standing before this magnificent home and, more specifically, from the tree where the ashes of the former owner lay in their final resting place…mixed with the earth beneath this tree. While outside, our psychic, Lisa, had *seen* the ashes of a man (the owner?) by one of the Tulip trees and stated, "But his spirit is not there."

This unusual waxed tulip flower was taken from the tree that shades the resting place of its former owner's ashes, buried beneath it.

Chapter Twelve:

HAUNTED CHURCHES?

THE REVEREND AND THE CHOIR SINGER

A famous unsolved murder of the 1920s was the Hall-Mills murder. Until the Lindbergh baby was kidnapped in 1932, this was the "Crime of the Century" — an Episcopal priest and a choirgirl lay dead beneath a crab apple tree. Who killed them?

Eleanor Mills was dressed in a red polka-dotted blue dress and black stockings. Her blue velvet hat lay beside her body. Around her

Gravesite of Eleanor Mills in Van Liew Cemetery. Take note of the orb in front and the blurriness... paranormal activity appears to abound here.
Courtesy of NJGO member Diane Finkel.

throat she wore a blood soaked, brown silk scarf. She lay stretched out at her lover's side, her left hand resting on his right knee. Rev. Hall's Panama hat covered his face and his right arm was under Eleanor's shoulder.

Eleanor was thirty-four years old and he was forty-one on this fateful September day in 1922. Leaning against the sole of his left shoe was his own business card and scattered between them were torn up letters and cards. He was the Reverend Edward W. Hall, pastor of the Episcopal Church of St. John the Evangelist in New Brunswick; his wife was Frances Noel Stevens, heiress to some Johnson and Johnson fortune. Eleanor Mills was a singer in the church choir and her husband the acting sexton at St. John's.

Dr. Hall and his choirgirl had a planned rendezvous on a Thursday evening for a romantic tryst beneath a crab apple tree on an abandoned farmland on the outskirts of town. The bodies weren't found until Saturday morning; by then her neck was crawling with maggots. He had been shot once over the right ear and she was shot three times in the right temple, under the right eye, and over the right ear. Her tongue had been cut out after she was shot and her choir singer's larynx removed.

A 32-caliber cartridge was found nearby and another bullet fell out of Hall's coat at the morgue. More bullets would be found at a later date, but first there would be one of the messiest, most scandalous, and most complicated murder cases in the history of the State of New Jersey.

The suspects were Hall's wife Frances Noel Stevens (1874-1942) and her two brothers, Henry Hewgill Stevens (1869-1939) and William "Willie" Carpender Stevens (1872-1942). The trial began November 3, 1926 in the Somerset County Courthouse in Somerville, New Jersey, with Charles W. Parker presiding as judge. The trial lasted about thirty days and garnered huge national attention in the newspapers and on radio, largely because of the social status of the wealthy Stevens and Carpender families.

The prosecution's key witness, Jane Gibson, was unreliable and changed details of the story each time she told it. Her account varied when told to the police, the newspapers, and in her trial testimony, which came from a hospital bed rolled into the courtroom. Frances Stevens Hall and her two brothers had the motive and the means for the murder, but there was not enough evidence to convict them.

The case was so confused and mismanaged, to the extent that the Ku Klux Klan was even rumored to have executed the couple for immoral acts. As a result, the case was all but dropped by 1926.

The gravesite of Eleanor Mills is located in the Van Liew Cemetery in New Brunswick, New Jersey, and the Reverend Hall is resting in Green-Wood Cemetery in Brooklyn, New York. It was nearing sunset when some NJGO members and I paid a visit to Eleanor. In doing so, we could not shake the strange feeling of stillness and the coldness surrounding the gravesite. A huge black crow seemed to appear from nowhere, landing on Eleanor's tombstone, and then flew off as quickly as it had appeared. After taking several photographs and making an attempt to contact Eleanor, we decided to move on to an adjacent cemetery that had been our main investigation location for that evening.

CRIES FROM THE PAST

St. James Church is located at 2136 Woodbridge Avenue in Edison. Emigrants from the area of Portsmouth, New Hampshire, settled this area in 1664. The burial ground that surrounds the church is not owned by the church, but by the city of Edison and holds the remains of many of the early settlers of the area, as well as troops that fought and died during the Revolutionary War. Some of the grave markers date back as early as 1693.

St. James Episcopal Church was established in 1704, but the Piscatawaytown Burial Ground much earlier. In 1835, the church was destroyed by a tornado and was rebuilt using as much of the original wood and fixtures as possible. The rear section was built in 1913. There was considerable military activity in the Piscatawaytown area in 1776 and 1777 and Woodbridge Avenue was a main land artery for British communications and movement of supplies and troops. The British army used St. James Church as a barracks and a hospital from December 1776 to June 1777, with several battles

An exterior view of the haunted, historic St. James Church...

The sign for the Piscatawaytown Burial Ground is located outside the fence of the cemetery property.

This is the early section of the cemetery as you first enter from the walkway leading to the church.

fought at, or very near to, the church. Located nearby is a common grave of British soldiers who had fallen in battle. They were buried in the British breastworks (defensive trench) that were emplaced along Post Road (now Woodbridge Avenue). At the request of the opposing Continental forces, the British also buried a number of Continental soldiers, but their resting place has been lost in time and is not known.

The Piscatawaytown Burial Ground is one of the earliest in Middlesex County and the oldest readable monument is dated 1693. There are many American soldiers buried from several wars and the highest-ranking veteran buried is Brevet Major General Thomas Swords, who was a veteran of both the Mexican War and Civil War. May all here be remembered and their sacrifices not lost in history.

When you consider the history of this location, one would be remiss to not have strong feelings of spirit energy when visiting the site or to see the occasional apparition. Visual sightings have been reported by locals and the occasional passerby, especially late at night and into the early hours of the morning. Since many wounded were brought into the church, it would seem possible that what some visitors believe is bloodstains are still visible on some of the pews.

Chapter Thirteen:
A HAUNTED MANSION

Lakeview, the historic Buckelew mansion located in Jamesburg, is twenty-two rooms and was home to Jamesburg's namesake, James Buckelew, and his family from 1832 to 1900. It was built in sections between 1685 and 1870, and the spirits at this more than 300-year-old mansion are not only active, but also protective of its heritage. Yet, the Buckelew Mansion is no roped-off museum, but rather a touchable time capsule that brings past centuries to life.

Ghostly Lakeview Mansion at night...

On one hot and humid June evening I accompanied NJGO on their investigation of the mansion. This was actually a joint investigation with another well-respected group, South Jersey Ghost Research, based in Philadelphia, Pennsylvania. Considering its past 'haunted' history, needless to say, we were not disappointed with our experiences.

When NJGO first arrived, the members of the South Jersey Ghost Research group were already there. This was to be a training exercise for a couple of new members of their group as well as a couple of new members of our own group. As we laid out our plan of operation, darkness began to set in and the mansion took on a completely different atmosphere. Splitting up into groups, we began setting up our equipment as we had three floors and a total of twenty-two rooms to cover that evening.

I first decided to venture into the room that housed the coach in which Abe Lincoln traveled to Trenton for an appearance. You can touch this piece of history and, *if the spirits will let you*, sit in the seat that the President once occupied. When repairs were nearing completion on the roof just above the Lincoln room, one of the workers lost his balance, his foot becoming tangled in one of the ropes that were being used, slipping and swinging to his death by crashing through the center window at the far end of the room.

However, let me warn you that when you're in the house and you pick up the family bible, the spirit of Mrs. Buckelew becomes very nervous and protective of it, so the sooner that you return it to its resting place the better. As an afterthought, it may be best if you do not touch it at all.

Opposite page, top:
The Lincoln coach is on display here and faces the window area where a worker met his demise.

Opposite page, bottom:
"Do not touch"... The family bible is watched over by the spirit of matriarch Mrs. Buckelew.

Chapter Fourteen:

HAUNTED THEATER IN PISCATAWAY

SPIRITED ENCORE

Tucked away on a secluded side street in Piscataway you will find the Circle Players Theater in the Round. Believed to have been built in the 1930s, this one-story structure has a basement that includes a kitchen area, restrooms, and three storage areas. It is primarily used as the main entrance for patrons, giving them access to the box office and a reception area before and after performances and during intermissions. The main level is the theater area that includes the performance floor, sound booth, and backstage area that houses the dressing, storage, and makeup rooms, as well as an attic.

The haunted Circle Players Theater... *Courtesy of Karen Timper.*

Having been occupied by the Circle Players Theater Group since 1971, at first glance the structure reminds one of a rural church or schoolhouse from days long past. You would be correct in this assumption because it was originally used as the Farmers Grange Hall, as indicated by a cornerstone of the building that reads P&H (Patrons of Husbandry) No. 152 and dated 1933. In subsequent years, a church and a schoolhouse occupied the building before finally being acquired by the Circle Players, which converted its use as the Theater in the Round.

The eerie setting of the theater lends itself as a doorway to the paranormal. From the very early days, American Indians roamed the property and there's one, having been hanged from a tree at the rear of the property, whose spirit still remains. He is a bit of a prankster who lightly tugs on the hair of the female actors. There is also the reverend of the church here — he was found by a caretaker after hanging himself on the upper landing outside the area now used by the actors as a dressing room — and the spirit of a young boy is occasionally seen in one of the seat rows. At times, a conversation can be heard in the foyer of the theater when no one is present.

Since 1971, there have been many experiences reported by the theater staff:

† Once, a director was resting on the downstairs couch and decided to stay there until his scheduled rehearsal time. He was awakened by the sounds of laughter and talking that sounded almost party-like. He assumed his actors were there, so he rushed upstairs… only to find that *no one* else was in the building.

† After all the rest of the theater members had gone outside, this same director had gone downstairs to turn off the lights and to close and lock the side lobby door. While he was down there, he heard what sounded exactly like furniture being repeatedly dragged across the stage upstairs. Everyone who was with him that evening knew that he was always afraid to be in the theater alone and so he had thought that they may have been trying to scare him, except for the fact that there was *no* furniture on the stage. It wasn't as if they could have come back in and made the sounds. The director had never been in the theater alone before

— *or since* — and to this day cannot rid himself of the creepy feeling from that evening.

† During a production of "Gemini" back in 1996, after one night's performance, a cast member was upstairs turning off the lights. There was only one other cast member in the building and they were downstairs by the box office. As the last light was turned off in the dressing room, the cast member felt a cold presence from behind that caused the hairs on the back their neck to stand erect. Swearing that they heard whispering coming from behind at just that same moment, the cast member bolted down the dressing room steps and into the lobby. When the other member saw him, the first thing he said was, "You just experienced our ghost, didn't you?" He had never experienced anything like it before and replied, "It was really freaky!"

† On another night, as the only member left upstairs was crossing the stage area to put a prop back on the prop table, he noticed that one of the swinging doors was open and the other one wasn't. As he stood at the prop table, the swinging door that was closed slowly began to open…as if someone was about to walk through it.

† One afternoon, as a cast member arrived at the theater to do some work, she heard two women talking, but had not noticed any other cars in the parking lot. To her, one of the voices sounded like one of the other members that she knew and someone else having a conversation and laughing. She moved in the direction of the voices, but when she opened the door there wasn't anyone there. After having this experience, she left the building, bewildered and a bit frightened.

† During one member's longevity with the theater, a number of unusual things have occurred from time to time, particularly in the stage area behind the six o'clock section and in the "Fozberry Room." This would be the small area that leads to the exit stairs into the parking lot. Their experiences included being called by name and going upstairs to see who was looking for him on several occasions when no one else was in the building — the member became quite use to it. One other time, while sitting in the lobby, he was reading a paperback copy of the *Exorcist*.

He began to quote a section he had just read that was different from that in the film and, just as he finished the quote, "Fear the priest," the book that he had placed on a coffee table flipped off and landed on the floor at his feet. This incident occurred in the presence of another cast member.

NJGO'S INVESTIGATION

Psychic Impressions

Lisa's Experience

NJGO conducted investigations at the theater on two separate occasions, at which yours truly was present. Psychic Lisa Palandrano was present during the first investigation; the following are her findings.

"Upon arriving at the location I was introduced to everyone inside and then proceeded outside to begin my external walk-around so as to not be influenced by any information coming from the discussion inside. I first went to the rear corner of the theater's yard area by the chairs and immediately sensed a woman figure with long gray hair, wearing a long flowing white gown. She was standing just behind me and seemed to be very excited that I was there. I asked her why she was here and she replied that she lives there. Curious, I asked her what she has done to people and her response was that she has tapped on people's hats and pulled and touched their hair. She continued by saying that she knows that she has passed over, but she likes it here; she likes the activity.

"Although it had rained earlier that evening, it had stopped for a brief time; however, drops of rain falling from the tree leaves were hitting my head and notepad. This was a sign to me that the tree spirit would talk to me. The tree spirit told me that there were lots of playful spirits here in the many vines … gnomes, fairies, and little people. The woman spirit jumped in and said that she goes in and out of the building, listening to the people. The tree spirit informed me that there are three spirits here: one lady and two men. The men are dressed in dark colored clothes with a 'T' type shirt of lighter color under their jackets and that they visit all around this area (the neighborhood). They have a second mission; to reassure people of the afterlife and that there is no hell. Both are very playful and will be staying here for a while yet.

"Inside the theater's dressing room, I asked if they were there (the three spirits mentioned to me outside) and I received a positive response. They actually sit in the dressing room and move items that are on the table! Asking what their names were, I received the names Gladys, Brady, and Warren. Gladys showed me the mist that she can use to float through the rooms and also informed me that they go through the front door when it is closed. After additional questioning, she said that they had lived in the area around 1800 and that the building has been used over and over again for different things. She said that she and one of the men loved to play act, while the other gentleman loved to create and write stories.

"Upon sitting in the main theater, I sensed a spirit — Gladys — immediately behind me. I asked for them (the spirits) to perform for those who were sitting in the dark, but she responded, "No, no, no... you are working!"

This spirit was felt behind Psychic Lisa Palandrano....

Jane's Experience

On a second investigation, NJGO returned with Psychic Jane Doherty, who began her walkthrough in the basement. After a brief introduction, Jane acclimated herself with the various rooms accompanied by Karen Timper, Pat Carpenter, and myself. I was tasked that evening with taking photographs during the entire walkthrough.

Left to right: NJGO Founder Karen Timper with Psychic Jane Doherty, who is discussing her initial feelings that she is receiving, and NJGO member Patrick Carpenter in the basement area of the Circle Players Theater.

Sitting on the sofa for a bit, Jane's immediate impression was that the structure had been built in the "gangster era." She also felt that the original structure had a section added on. Her next impression was that a murder (a male victim by stabbing) had taken place in close proximity to the back of the theater (on the street) either in the 1950s or 1960s, but more likely in the 1950s. In the 1930s, a man committed suicide (by hanging) in the building. She also indicated that when she first arrived, she had seen a man in the basement near the restroom area.

Renowned Psychic Jane Doherty is experiencing strong spirit energy during her initial walkthrough of the dressing rooms.

Taking the narrow staircase near the restroom area, we made our way up to the main theater level in the area of the dressing room. Immediately Jane felt the presence of a spirit that was eluding her and, when she stood in this area, her *psychic stomach* reacted. She followed a specific path where her stomach stayed continually distended. This path led us from the middle of the makeup counter to the doorway that leads into the stage area, closest to the narrow staircase. This area presents one with a very strong feeling of oppression...the same kind that Jane related feeling on the third floor of the William Heath Davis House in San Diego, California, and the creepiness, lurking, peeking, and watching in the cellar of the Lizzie Borden home in Fall River, Massachusetts.

Jane also brings attention to the fact that when you are alone in the building, you should hear footsteps, as she sees the same man that she saw in the basement area earlier. This spirit enjoys walking around in various areas of the theater. The gentleman is a caretaker, holding a lantern or something similar while he walks up the narrow staircase. She describes him as an older man, approximately 5'10", and a big man who moves methodically, shuffling his feet as he walks. It was he who came upon the suicide victim in the dressing room area, which is believed to have been that of a minister back when the structure was used as a church. Jane made a comparison of this general area to that of an altar area of a church that extended to the platform rows of seating that now fronts the area.

Moving into the theater area, Jane sat in the top row of seats immediately in front of the dressing room area wall. She began to feel that the theater's floor (performing area) was giving off a different type of energy — a peaceful, comfortable, light energy. This, in part, may have been due to the theater's stage lighting that encompasses the ceiling and referencing the fact that the heat from the various lamps can change the energy for the spirits.

At this juncture of the walkthrough, Jane received the names Harold (Harry), Charles, Leonard, and Jack. She saw two of the male spirits wearing dark colored Quaker-type clothing. After making this final point of interest, the walkthrough essentially concluded; however, as we ascended the second narrow staircase at the foyer end

Jane also received spirit energy while sitting in the main theater area...

of the stage area and walked toward the area of the box office, once again Jane's *psychic stomach* began to extend and she saw a female bending down, tending to something that resembled a garden, perhaps outside!

Q & A Dialogue

Through the use of a pendulum, the following conversation was conducted in the dressing room area with the spirit of the American Indian that still lingers in the theater. I am certain that you will find it most interesting. Using my pendulum to obtain responses to my questions, I recorded the session on my digital recorder so that I would have a record of the dialogue.

Foyer — 5:48 p.m.
Is there anyone present who wishes to speak with me tonight? If you wish to speak with me and your answer is 'yes', please make the

instrument I'm holding (pendulum) rotate in a circular motion. If your answer is 'no', then make the instrument swing back and forth.

Q. Do you wish to speak to me tonight? …
A. No.
Q. I'm not here to do you any harm. I would just like to communicate with you. The instrument I'm holding is called a pendulum and you can use it to communicate with me. Is there anyone here who wishes to speak to me? …
A. Yes.
Q. Are you a man? …
A. No.
Q. Are you a female? …
A. Yes.
Q. Are you a young woman? …
A. Yes.
Q. Have you been here for a while? …
A. No.
Q. Is there anyone else with you? …
A. Yes.
Q. Is the person with you a man? …
A. Yes.
Q. Is the man related to you? …
A. Yes.
Q. How long has the man been here? (*No response.*) A year? …
A. No.
Q. More than ten years? …
A. Yes.
Q. More than fifty years? (*The spirit hesitates.*) Is the man your husband? …
A. Yes.
Q. Do you feel comfortable speaking with me? …
A. Yes.
Q. Does the male presence wish to speak with me now? …
A. Yes.

I direct the next question to the male presence.

Q. Have you been here more than ten years? …
A. Yes.

A brief break occurs in the dialogue.

Q. Do you wish to resume our conversation? …
A. Yes. (The response could have been from either or from both.)
Q. Have either of you been here more that one hundred years? …
A. No.
Q. Do either of you realized that you have passed on? …
A. Yes.
Q. Is this response from the female? …
A. Yes.
Q. Was your passing due to an accident? …
A. Yes.
Q. Did the accident occur here? …
A. Yes.
Q. In this building? …
A. Yes.
Q. As a theater? …
A. Yes.
Q. When this was a Grange? …
A. No.
Q. Did the accident occur less than fifty years ago? …
A. Yes.
Q. Did the accident occur in this building? …
A. Yes.
Q. Was this a theater at the time? …
A. No. (This is a conflicting response since the spirit previously indicated it had been a theater.)
Q. Is this the woman I'm speaking with? …
A. Yes.

Q. Are you twenty-five years old? …
A. Yes.
Q. Are you fifty years old? …
A. No.
Q. Are you thirty years old? …
A. No.
Q. Are you twenty-five years old? …
A. Yes.
Q. Did the accident occur fifty years ago? …
A. Yes.
Q. Was the year 1950? …
A. No.
Q. Was it in 1960? …
A. No.
Q. Was the year 1952? …
A. No.
Q. Then it was 1950? …
A. Yes, but with a hesitation.
Q. Was it in 1956? …
A. Yes, but a weak response.
Q. Was the year 1955? …
A. No.
Q. Was it in 1957? …
A. No.
Q. The accident occurred in 1955? …
A. Yes. (Conflicting response)
Q. Was there a vehicle involved in the accident? …
A. Yes.
Q. Was there a horse involved in the accident? …
A. No.
Q. Were you in the vehicle? …
A. No.
Q. Were you standing on this property? …
A. The spirit hesitates.
Q. Were you in the roadway? …
A. Yes.

I thank you both for speaking with me this evening and you are welcome to remain here as your presence is welcomed by those who presently inhabit this location.

Dressing Room — 6:26 p.m.

If any spirits are present, the instrument that I'm holding is a pendulum. It will not harm you and you may use it to communicate with me by responding to my questions with a yes or no reply. If your reply is 'no', make the pendulum swing back and forth. If your reply is 'yes', please swing the pendulum in a circular motion.

Q. Is there anyone here who wishes to communicate with me this evening? ...

A. No.

Q. Are you afraid to speak with me? ...

A. No.

Q. Is there any reason that you wish not to communicate with me tonight? ...

No response.

Q. Are you afraid of me? ...

A. Yes.

Q. You don't have to be afraid of me. I'm not going to hurt you...I just want to find out who you are, possibly why you are here, and if you are friendly. Are you friendly? ...

A. Yes.

Q. Is there anyone else here with you tonight? ...

No response.

Q. If you don't mind, let me ask you one more question: Can you see me? ...

A. Yes.

Q. Are you a man? ...

A. Yes.

Q. Are you a woman? ...

A. No.

Q. Are you part of the theater group? ...

A. No.

Q. Were you here when this building was a school? ... *Spirit is hesitating.*

Q. Were you here when this building was a Grange? ...
Spirit is hesitating again.

Q. Are you more than fifty years old? ...

A. *Yes.* (But the spirit seems to hesitate a little.)

Q. Are you still afraid to speak with me? ...

A. *Yes.*

Q. Are you more than fifty years old? ...

A. *Yes.* (Yes, it was a repeat question, but I received a more positive response).

Q. Are you more than one hundred years old? ...

A. *Yes.*

Q. Do you mean that you were here more than one hundred years ago? ...

A. *Yes.*

Q. Did you belong to an Indian Tribe? ...

A. *Yes.*

Q. Is there anyone else here with you this evening? ...

A. *Yes.*

Q. Do you realize that you have passed on? ...

A. *Yes.*

Q. Are you trying to communicate with people here? ...

A. *Yes.*

Q. Do you pull people's hair? ...

A. *Yes.*

Q. Do you do this often? ...

A. *Yes.*

Q. Do you push people? ...

A. *No.*

Q. Do you make sounds or make noises? ...

A. *Yes.*

Q. Are you happy here? ...

A. *Yes.*

Q. Do you wish to leave here? ...

A. *No.*

A strange noise is noted at 9:25 p.m. on my voice recorder.

Q. Did you die at this location? …
A. Yes.
Q. Was there an accident? …
A. No.
Q. Were you killed here? …
A. No.
Q. Did you die of natural causes? …
A. No.
Q. Was there anyone responsible for your death? …
The spirit hesitates. Whoever this is seems confused.
Q. You indicated that you're an American Indian or an Indian. Is that true? …
A. Yes.
Q. Was there a battle of some sort here? …
A. No.
Q. You indicated that the person with you is a male. Is that true? …
The spirit started to say yes, then went to no. It seems to be confused again.
Q. Do you know where you are? …
A. No. (But the spirit seems confused again.)
Q. Why are you so confused? Is it because you don't know what happened to you? …
The spirit hesitates, going back and forth.
Q. Does this other individual with you wish to speak with me? …
A. No.
Q. Are you in need of any help? …
A. Yes, but with hesitation.
Q. Is there a way that we can help you? …
A. Yes.
Q. You said that you want to stay here. Is that true? … *A. Yes.*
Q. You're happy here. Is that true? …

A. Yes.

Q. You just want to remain here and harm no one. Is that correct?
   (*Once again the spirit hesitates, but I'm going to take it as a yes.*)

Q. Can you see me? ...

A. Weak hesitation.

Q. Can you make your presence known in another way? ...

A. No.

The dialogue concludes there, but hopefully I will be able to talk again later with this spirit.

Summary

On October 24-25, 2008, the Circle Players presented their annual Halloween Hair-Raiser 2 and one of their presentations was titled "Observances," written and directed by John Dowgin. The cast members were Syndi Szabo, John Pizzigoni, Joyce Porter, Illark Alcaro, and Pat Carpenter.

The technical aspects of the investigations, although important, are not paramount to the insights of NJGO's psychics, the photographic evidence, and the conclusions of the investigations. Attending the first investigation were Linda Condrillo, a reporter from the *Westfield Leader*, and Augusto F. Menezes, a staff photographer from the *Home News Tribune*.

It is no surprise that haunting activity is actively present when you consider all of the contributing circumstances that opened these paranormal doors. Based on the physical, scientific, photographic, and psychic evidence that NJGO experienced and captured, which members of the theater group had also experienced, even the most ardent skeptic would have to concede that the Circle Player's Theater is most definitely HAUNTED!

Chapter Fifteen:

HAUNTINGS IN THE HALL

Shown is the Author standing by the entrance sign to Marlboro Psychiatric Hospital. *Courtesy of Karen Timper.*

Marlboro Psychiatric Hospital is located on Route 520 just a short distance after crossing Route 79 in Marlboro, New Jersey. Run by the State of New Jersey, it first opened in the early 1930s. Set in a rural environment, the hospital campus was about four hundred plus acres. The hospital closed in 1998 following a 1993 undercover investigation that found rampant patient abuse, wasteful spending, and other illegal practices.

Since its 1998 closing, the abandoned hospital has become the focus of numerous local legends. The hospital buildings themselves are said to be haunted and security at the buildings has been tightened to deter trespassers. Shadow people are alleged to have been seen on the grounds at various times.

Screams once echoed in the night from within these walls, voiced by those driven mad by their own demons. Those damned were housed in this man-made purgatory, locked away from decent folk, out of sight and out of mind. Yet, though the windows are boarded and the hallways empty, something lingers. Screams are still heard without the benefit of mouths to shape them, footsteps tread without legs attached, and around any corner a foul wind blows, its stench turning the stomach and driving the curious away. Though it has been abandoned for many years, not all of the patients seem to have left.

My daughter Karen, the founder of NJGO, and I recently paid a visit to this remnant of the past in hopes of gaining entrance or, at the very least, to photograph some of the buildings. In speaking with one of the security guards, we were informed that from time to time young people infiltrate the grounds, holding rituals in hopes of raising the dead. We were told that, especially after dark, when the security guard is walking the grounds during his periodic rounds, an eerie feeling is felt as the atmosphere seems to change and one hastens to leave.

According to legend, the land originally contained a slaughterhouse and cattle farm. The story goes that the owner refused to sell until the town simply seized the land, with the owner himself eventually becoming a patient in the hospital. Whether or not the story is true, the fact remains that in 1933 the quiet town of Marlboro saw the construction of this massive psychiatric hospital, which, when completed, covered nearly five hundred acres. The finished compound contained an administration building, administration cottages, a greenhouse, and many patient cottages, some of which held upward to fifty-five inmates.

At its height, the hospital contained 670 beds and employed well over 1,300 staff and doctors. However, what began as a home for the disturbed took a macabre turn when reports of abuse and neglect began to circulate and the death toll began to rise. Across from the main gate is a small section of land that was set aside as a cemetery for those who died while undergoing care in the early days. It also wasn't long before the beds were full…yet patients continued arriving at a high rate.

The patients who were treated at Marlboro ranged from the slightly troubled to those with deep psychotic tendencies. As the years passed, more of the latter began making their homes on the grounds, some wandering in the open fields and many times escaping. In 1984, 151 escapes by inmates and patients prompted the surrounding community residents to acquire a record number of handguns and to file legal action against the state for the very existence of the hospital. A formal investigation was scheduled and the findings were extensive. The patients, according to official police reports, were treated with less rights and respect than prisoners, with many of them suffering from malnutrition.

As conditions worsened and the investigations continued, it became very clear that something was wrong at the hospital and no amount of restructuring would be able to undo the damage done. Beginning in July 1995 and over the next three years, nearly eight hundred patients were moved out of the aging structure…bringing relief to some, but terror to those who knew that some of them would be set free.

The Ghosts

Due to the number of deaths and the great amount of suffering and tragedy that occurred within the walls of Marlboro Psychiatric Hospital, there is no way of knowing how many of the restless souls still wander the hallways. What is known, however, is that *something* remains, as people who have entered the buildings have experienced much phenomena.

Urban explorers and ghost hunting groups have reported hearing phantom footsteps and the sounds of animals, such a pigs and cows, when none are present, perhaps harkening back to the days of the slaughter house. Others report hearing screaming or giggling from empty rooms, and there is certainly no shortage of EVP recordings to come out of the buildings. Most disturbing, however, is the sudden onset of a gut-churning stench that is often accompanied by cold spots and the sensation of being touched.

Across the road from the security entrance is a narrow tree-covered dirt road that leads to a tiny cemetery. Many patients who died while at Marlboro are now at peace. The unusual part about this burial place is its headstones. Made of stamped tin, most stand crooked and rusting and only exhibiting the patient's identification number. The patients remained in oblivion, as their names were never placed on the headstones, and in recent years this has caused much controversy with relatives searching for loved ones and having difficulty in locating their graves.

The patient cemetery... Many of the tortured souls of the institution lay in rest here. *Courtesy of Karen Timper.*

This rusted stamped tin headstone depicts only a number for the deceased patient. *Courtesy of Karen Timper.*

Since some buried here had been deemed by a local veterans organization as having been veterans of various wars, the State was forced to build a structure housing the corresponding names to the numbers so that visitors could easily locate the gravesites of those who had long passed from their midst.

For the paranormal investigator, keep in mind that "rust" is known to possess the capability to record past happenings and to replay the scene when atmospheric conditions are right. It may be possible for one to venture into a "time warp or time tear" in areas such as this. *(For more on time warps, see Chapter 23.)*

The Present Day

Today the institution sits, empty and foreboding, a wasteland of boarded up buildings and overgrown fields, simply a mirror in time awaiting some miracle to erase the pain endured there during its many years of existence. Very few are aware of the labyrinth of tunnels that wind their way beneath the compound, reaching out to every building and beyond. We were informed that there is about half a foot of water in the tunnels and, unless you mark your path, you could easily become lost and may never find your way out.

I can recall back in the early 1970s, while employed as an outside sales representative for a large film company, making periodic visits to the hospital's print shop as they were one of my accounts. On one of my visits, I was privy to see the beginning of one of

One of the main buildings as it stands today... Eerie looking with windows boarded and broken, the building is still home to the spirited inhabitants of yesteryear. *Courtesy of Karen Timper.*

the tunnels that I had heard whispers about and where missing patients were occasionally found wandering aimlessly. Even just walking the hallways, I received strange glances from the patients; occasionally one would utter the words "take me out of here" to me. It felt unusually strange for me just to be there, knowing that I could at least walk out and return home to my family when my mission was completed.

I never experienced anything unusual, though there was a feeling of despair that seemed to permeate the air. One cannot imagine the many phases of trauma that some of the residents must have endured on a daily basis. However, thinking back to those days, I do recall having unusual feelings and always thinking that something other than the patients was watching me and was always happy for me to leave. My sixth sense was most likely kicking in, but at the time I did not realize it. Even today I wonder if some of those wandering the grounds and hallways were physical human beings or were they just visiting from the other realm — or maybe they had never left.

Today, the grounds are off limits to the general public, mainly for safety reasons, due to the fact that when the institution was initially constructed asbestos was used in most of the buildings. Considering the enormous health risk by just walking into some of the buildings, you may encounter a dust storm of this toxic material. Hopefully, one day the state may consider refurbishing one of the buildings, preferably the hospital building and opening it to ghost hunting groups and members of the general public. I am certain that by doing this it would raise revenue for the state instead of being a complete and unproductive wasteland. However, you can still pay your respects to the patient cemetery across the road. Who knows? You might just experience a bit of the past from some of the souls that wander there, still at unrest.

Chapter Sixteen:

A CLASSIC HAUNTING — OR IS IT?

This scenario takes place in a private home in a northwestern section of Central New Jersey. I had the opportunity of participating in this investigation with NJGO. For obvious reasons, the exact location and the family's name have been kept confidential.

Settlement of the area where the home is located began as early as 1664 and included Scottish Quakers and second-generation immigrants from the New England states. The first inhabitants were Native American Indians, particularly from the Lenape Tribes. Situated between the towns of Edison and Middlesex, this area saw extensive skirmishing during the Revolutionary War. The skirmish named Dismal Swamp occurred May 17, 1777 and would most likely have encompassed the housing development area in which this home sits, as it would have been swampland prior to any development.

The family reported the following phenomena:

† The smell of flowers during winter months.
† Sounds of someone walking across the second floor when no one else was at home, as heard by the husband; the incident prompted him to leave.
† Colder temperatures noticed in the living room and specifically in the area of the couch.
† Almost at the same time each night (3-4 a.m.), their then eighteen-month-old child is woken up standing in his crib and yelling, "No, no, no!" Usually the episodes last approximately a minute or so and is apparently caused by his hearing or seeing a spirit.
† A toy truck and kitchen blender have turned on for no apparent reason.

However, the strangest phenomena of all is that in occasional photographs taken of the child, a bluish coloration to his lips might be seen in one photo, but not in the prior one or the one after. And at times a blackish-blue ooze appears to be coming from within the child's mouth in a photograph that is not visible to the human eye. Only in these photographs is the presence of an orb near the child. This condition has been discussed with the child's pediatrician, and although the parents thought that it could be "paranormal," this was not discussed with the doctor, who did not feel that the condition was anything to be medically concerned with.

NJGO'S INVESTIGATION

On this investigation, the group had two psychics present; however, before their arrival I encountered the presence of latent energy with the use of my pendulum in the bathroom next to the child's bedroom and in the south side of the master bedroom. It was noted that when the latent energy was detected in the master bedroom, it was no longer present in the bathroom and would appear that the energy was moving to different locations.

In an interview with the child's parents, it was disclosed that the child was born on the anniversary of the father's maternal grandmother's death. The child's great-grandmother's last word before she passed was "apple" — and this was the child's very first spoken word!

Psychic Impressions

Lisa's Experience

"I saw a grandmother Native American spirit who still stays with him (the child in another lifetime). I saw a fire pit; he was about twelve or so and his name then was Eagleson and he was honored and much cared for.

"In another lifetime, I saw two spirits with him and once again he was a boy. A slice to the neck caused his death in that lifetime that had taken place around the time of Buddha. I would not be surprised if he (the child) grew up to teach about things that he would not normally have been taught in this lifetime."

(Lisa's impressions were validated, as it was confirmed later that the family has Native American Indian ties.)

Jane's Experience

All of the team members felt an extreme coldness in the living room when the opening prayer was being delivered and psychic Jane Doherty's *paranormal stomach* reacted. There was a low interruption on the electromagnetic field detector, and Jane's stomach also reacted as she approached a corner in the child's bedroom and again in the master bedroom. During the course of the day, the child gravitated to this corner that he apparently felt to be a safe spot to play.

Since the intensity level of this investigation was so high, I feel that by presenting Jane's full psychic report it will better explain the impact this investigation had on all the team members who were present.

I arrived at the house, parked my car directly across the street, and, as I exited the car, I began immediately scanning the energy of the home in relationship to the other houses. My first impression indicated that there was a break in the energy field of the houses. Instead of an energy field flowing harmoniously from home to home, the energy seemed to break on both sides of the house that I would be investigating. This indicated to me that the energy of the house was isolated from the others and also indicated there was a good possibility that the house had some discarnate energy as had previously been reported.

Next, I scanned the street area to determine if I received any impressions that may indicate "problem energy" on the street that may affect the activity in the house. I kept focusing on the area of a house or two from the house we were investigating and, as I tried to determine why I centered my attention on that area, I received a vision of a car crash. As I focused more, it became clear there was an accident that had taken place on the street and in that accident someone had died. As I keyed in more, I received an image of a young teenage boy walking on the street and being hit by a car. My first reaction to this image was that it could have something to do with the reported activity in the home I was about to enter.

I entered the home and was introduced to the little boy and his parents. There was a lot of activity and the team was already there, taking readings and talking to the family. This gave me the opportunity to observe everyone for any impressions that could give me a clue as to what was going on with the boy. Before entering the house and hearing the details, I was concerned that this could be some type of possession, so I wanted to handle it carefully and key into my impressions before allowing my stomach to search for the spirit's energy spots.

I observed the boy's interaction with members of the team, as well as the parents' reactions, and noticed nothing that was out of the ordinary. I carefully studied the boy and concluded that his energy field did not indicate that there was anything malevolent around him. I observed his parents while they were interacting with the team members and telling me what they had observed in the house. Again there were no impressions that they had an energy field that was contributing to the activity. I did not sense implanted thought forms in the house nor any unusual violent activity that could have happened in the house. There was no pent-up psychokinetic energy in either parent. These initial impressions helped me to let my guard down and proceed with my walkthrough. If I had sensed strong negative energy, I would have had to carefully protect myself and would have done so before I entered the other rooms. My psychic tools — my crystal skulls — would have been held over my head and I would have brought God's energy into me for greater protection to do whatever I had to do to release the spirit if necessary.

My stomach reaction is the "tool" I use to locate spirit energy fields and the path of a spirit in a haunted situation. For some odd reason, when I am near a spirit, my stomach expands anywhere from three to five inches. There is no medical reason for the phenomenon and I can only offer the explanation that the "gut" area was where the third eye was located in ancient days. Today we refer to our third eye as being in our mind and in the space between our two eyes. There is a physical sensation in everyone's body that will react to psychic information. For me, it is my "gut" and it is a pronounced and very visible reaction. Over the years, I have grown to trust this reaction as accurate simply because it has been uncannily accurate in pinpointing where a person has had an encounter with spirit energy.

I scanned the living room, but I found no remarkable spirit energy inhabiting the area that concerned me. Occasionally *it* could enter that room, but I didn't feel that it was the "spirit hang out" that I was looking for.

The next room I scanned was the young boy's room and there I found the path of the spirit being...the area that was the "spirit hang out." My stomach reacted right by the closet door on the right side of the boy's crib (if you looked at it as you walked in the door). I knew this was the major spot in the room where the spirit roamed the most as soon as I physically reacted. I next walked around the crib to determine the full path of the spirit and my stomach continued to react as I walked in front of the crib. As soon as I got to the area at the end of the crib, the contractions and gripping sensations in my stomach were released and I was able to conclude that this is the active spirit area.

Next, I tried to determine the emotions attached to the spirit energy and felt the energy to be protective and again not harmful. At the same time, I felt as though it could be possessing, but not as a true possession. It was as if the spirit was protecting and not leaving the child. The first impression could have made me feel that it may be a possession, but the energy was too protective for it to be one. My impression of the energy told me it belonged to a female person and at that point I knew it wasn't the spirit I had first sensed of the teenage boy killed on the street or in an accident. In my mind, I had the lingering question of whether it could be a relative of the family.

The parents then offered some information that I psychically resonated with. When the boy was born, he had a major health problem and almost died. He still was plagued with severe allergies. Now, here is the part I don't remember...exactly what he had when he was born, but the information about his grandmother made me feel it was definitely his deceased grandmother who was around him acting as a guardian and protecting him. His grandmother lets the family know she is around by showing herself in pictures in the form of the color blue to his lips and once I concluded my impressions with that determination my stomach released in the way I usually feel it to do so when I have an accurate impression. Whether this reaction is caused by my own guide confirming my observation or if it is the spirit letting me know it is the right observation cannot be delineated at this point. It doesn't really concern me which it is…just that it is!

I proceeded into the parent's bedroom and found my stomach reacting near the bed on the window side. I felt that the energy was male and received the feeling that the young boy killed on the street, or who may have previously lived on the street and was killed in a car crash, does enter the room at times. However, I did not feel this spirit was the one centered on the child and that it was separate from the activity that was.

Upon closer observation, I discovered that the father of the child had some Tibetan artifacts on a table under that window and observed that one or two of these artifacts had spirits attached to them. They were not threatening or harmful, so I dismissed the artifacts as having anything to do with the activity around the child.

The activity surrounding the child was definitely that of his grandmother protecting him especially because of his previous health issues, some of which he still has. My concluding impressions indicated that she shows herself in pictures as the color blue on his lips and that she wants the family to know that she is protecting him from the other side. Perhaps this was her way of trying to let them know that he will be okay and that they could relax because, from the other side, she was around him all the time protecting him. The fact that she can show herself in pictures as the color blue on his lips may also be happening because she can use the energy of other spirits in the house to help her manifest in this way.

Chapter Seventeen:

HAUNTING BOYHOOD MEMORIES

GHOSTS WALKING THE BOARDS?

I can recall as a young boy making frequent visits to Asbury Park with my parents and then in the 1950s and 1960s with my own children. What a great place to spend the day; a beach resort complete with boardwalk, amusements, rides, and plenty of good places to eat. What more could a kid ask for except for possibly a ghost or two? At the time I was not aware of the paranormal or all that it entailed.

Asbury Park, in its heyday during the early part of the twentieth century, was host to men in derby hats and women in long dresses carrying parasols while walking the boards and basket type conveyances carrying those who became tired from walking and wanted to ride back, being pushed helter-skelter along the boards. These conveyances still existed in my day and I can picture them in my mind, hearing the rumbling of the wheels as they hit the separations between the boards. The stretch of beach being crowded had never changed from the early times to my visits there in the middle of the same century. Toward the latter part of the twentieth century, Asbury Park gradually became a "Ghost Town": the amusements disappeared along with most of the businesses and the town began to deteriorate with buildings being boarded up and very few people frequenting the area. The once active strip of beach was empty and eerie feelings overcame those who did venture there.

However, during the twentieth century, Asbury Park was firmly established among New Jersey's foremost seashore resorts, vying with Cape May, Atlantic City, and nearby Long Branch for visitors. Asbury Park sparkled with the presence of five-and-dime czar Frank W. Woolworth, Jazz great Duke Ellington, adventure-travel writer Lowell Thomas, Pulitzer Prize-winning York City mayor Ed Koch, bandleader Arthur Pryor, whose composition "Whistler and His Dog" became the theme song for TV's "Leave It to Beaver," Olympic track hopeful Frank Budd, actors Bud Abbott, Danny DeVito, and Jack Nicholson, big-band trumpeter Harry James, actor and Civil Rights crusader Canada Lee, award-winning poet Margaret Widdemer, NAACP founder W.E.B. DuBois, crooner Frank Sinatra, and teacher Elizabeth Gray Vining, whose autobiography was turned into the movie "The King and I."

There is a leering clown face that is a vivid reminder of the boardwalk's past glory. Bruce Springsteen fans are hoping that someone will rescue the mural and clown face on the side of the old Palace amusement arcade, as Bruce once posed with Tillie the Clown in a promo photo. The arcade has been slated for demolition since part of its interior collapsed some time ago, but in days gone by the Palace once contained two great spook rides — an elaborate fun house and a huge ferris wheel that extended upward through an opening in the roof. Today the Asbury Park oceanfront is a bleak no-man's land of closed businesses and stymied development dreams. Bruce Springsteen lives nowhere near this area, but he still performs there sometimes. When you least expect him, he will show up at the Stone Pony Club.

Are spirits of days passed still waking the boards, frolicking on the sandy stretch of beach, or standing by a vacant eatery, smelling the hotdogs, popcorn, and cotton candy that still permeates the air? Are they riding a now non-existent amusement ride? Can you still hear the eerie sounds of the carnival-like music being played as you walk the boards? On some secluded stretches of beach, you may hear voices whispering in the German language of submarine sailors who casually came ashore during the wee hours of the morning on many a non-moonlit night during the Second World War.

To elaborate a bit on the "submarine" scenario, the father of a high school friend of my wife's and I was a member of the German Bund that was located here in northern New Jersey during the World War II years. Part of his duties was that once a month he and one or two other members would head towards a pre-designated location on a lonely stretch of sand at Asbury Park or nearby sometime after the hour of midnight. This stealth operation was to meet a German submarine at a specific time and to help with the inflatable raft from the sub that would come ashore under the cloak of darkness, bringing with it a few of the crew members to afford them the opportunity to spend the next day or two lounging on the warm sunny beaches at Asbury Park, intermingling with the American civilian population that flocked to the resort during the summer months. Also coming ashore each time were one or two non-crewmembers who would not be returning, as they were here for clandestine operations, spying, or other unknown reasons! As difficult as it may be to believe, this operation was never discovered and continued almost until the war's end. Area residents never really knew just how vulnerable our coastline was to infiltration during this wartime period, but now there is an easy way for you to find out — you will just have to go there! You might just have a firsthand experience of your own or be privy to a paranormal treat, possibly a residual haunting of those long but really not forgotten days to one or more of the spirits…some that wander back to a more peaceful time.

I would not recommend staying too long after sunset, but if you do plan on visiting the spirits at Asbury Park, do not forget to bring along your camera and a digital voice recorder. Maybe the spirits will pose for you or implant a message on your recorder…that is, if you respect them and speak to them nicely.

However, I am happy to say that Asbury Park is on an upward trend and trying to rebuild and regain its former atmosphere as a resort area. I am certain the spirits appreciate it; I know that I do.

THE CABIN IN THE WOODS

In 1949, in Branchville, New Jersey, there was a place called Kamp Kiamesha, now referred to as Old K.K. by the "old timers, camp alumni." At the time, the Y.M.C.A. of Newark operated this camp and it was my first year being able to attend. My first view of the camp was the stone entranceway as my father drove his 1931 Chevrolet up the dirt road leading to a small wooded area. To my amazement, this wooded area opened to a huge field that was surrounded on three sides with wood platform tents and a large mess hall. At the bottom right corner of the field, which had a slight downward slope, you could

Above: The "Old K.K" as it stands today… *ghostly and foreboding*. **Below**: This once was the proud entrance to the "Old K.K." Now in deteriorating condition, still standing are two lonely sentries. The name Kamp Kiamesha that once spanned them has fallen victim to the ages. *Courtesy of former Kiameshian Tom Crosby.*

see the magnificent lake and a rickety old swimming dock and boat launching area. This "boys only" paradise was nestled in the Kittatinny Mountains that was a long ridge across northwestern New Jersey and Eastern Pennsylvania of the Delaware Valley.

Since this was my first time at camp and away from home by myself, and only being there for a two-week stay, things seemed a bit intimidating. I was assigned to the Junior row of tents. There was an Intermediate row and a Senior row for boys of different age groups. The eerie part were the ghost stories and legends told at the evening campfires, including the one about Tom Quick...

> The lake was given the name "Quick Pond" after the legendary Tom Quick. The legend goes that in 1756 while Thomas Quick, one of his sons, and his son-in-law were working by the river farming or cutting wood for their mill, they were attacked by Indians from the nearby woods. The Quicks had no weapons and ran for their lives for the house. The elder Quick was heavy and about the age of sixty-six, so his sons grabbed him by the arms and tried to hurry him along as he begged the boys to abandon him and flee. A bullet wounded one of the sons and the boys at last had to leave their father. The boys barely escaped by crossing the frozen Delaware River into New Jersey, but they were still at a position to be able to see the Indians kill and scalp the elder Quick and cut a pair of silver buckles from his trousers. One of his sons was Tom Quick and he pledged he would revenge the death of his father. He was about twenty-two years old at the time and years later he was able to get the buckle back after killing a number of Indians in cold blood. Legend has it that he killed over one hundred Indians.

Haunting in appearance is Quick Pond's swimming area as seen from the old boathouse launching dock. *Courtesy of former Kiameshian Tom Crosby.*

It was not until several years later, when I began attending Old K.K. for a month during my summer vacation from school, that I had my own personal experience. The belief was that Tom Quick's ghost still roamed the surrounding hills in search of Indians. True or not, another boy and I were about to find out for ourselves and, in the process, we came across something we never expected!

On one warm, sunny morning, the camp director, "Moose" Wands, gave us permission to go on a hike by ourselves, so we stopped by the mess hall kitchen to see "old Walt," the head cook, to see if we might get some food to take along with us since we would be missing lunch. Walt gave us a loaf of bread and a jar of peanut butter — "the old kid's staple" — that would keep us going until we returned for the evening meal. We filled our canteens with water and began our journey.

Passing the rifle range, we began our upward climb to our first stop that was known as "Bald Rock," a huge rock formation that could easily be seen from the camp below. Climbing a bit higher, we followed the trail along the mountain ridge and then began our trek downward toward what we believed to be the middle of the lake area. Then we would follow what we hoped would be a trail alongside the lake back to camp. The trees seemed to become larger and taller, blocking out the sun and making the woods darker. We had forgotten to bring along a watch, so we didn't know what time it was. As a result, we not only lost track of time, but we got lost!

Finally, we came across a small cabin that was seemingly broken down with age. An eerie feeling overtook us. Nervously, I began to approach the front door when, suddenly, out of nowhere I began to hear what I can only explain as a humming or buzzing type of noise. A thought flashed through my mind and I was overwhelmed with the feeling that something or someone was warning me that I must get out of here as quickly as possible. Immediately we started moving in the direction where we felt the lake was. After a few feet, I turned my head for another quick look at the cabin — *it was no longer there!* It just seemed to have disappeared.

Knowing what I do now about the paranormal, I believe that what I experienced was a "time warp," but what a story we had to tell around many campfires to come. We finally did make it back to camp and just in time for the evening meal.

Above: This view, looking toward the mess hall as it stands today, was taken from the dock area. **Below**: This ghost-like view was taken through a window of the deteriorating interior of "Old K.K.'s" mess hall... spirits of past campers may still remain there. *Courtesy of former Kiameshian Tom Crosby.*

I don't know if anyone who visits the camp will ever have this type of experience, but the remnants of the tents are no longer present, although some of the other buildings are. A dock and boathouse area are deteriorating and in a partially collapsed state. Should you decide to pay a visit to Old K.K., you may still encounter something unusual from days past.

OLYMPIC PARK'S HAUNTING PAST

Run by the Guenther family, Olympic Park was bordered by Maplewood and Newark and was in existence from 1887 to 1965. It featured the Whirl Wind that was a 1924 John Miller coaster that ran until it was blown down by a hurricane in 1950. The following year Herb Schmeck designed the Jet that was a compact coaster John Allen raved about. He said, "For the small plot of land it occupied, in my opinion it was the finest roller coaster ever built."

The park also had a rare John Miller Dip-Lo-Docus that featured riding in a "tea-cup" like car grafted onto a mild coaster layout. The park closed due to growing problems that many urban parks faced, as a few publicized acts of violence worked to keep the important family base away. Fortunately one important piece of Olympic Park survived to give pleasure to future generations — the park's PTC carousel from 1914 was restored and moved to Walt Disney World where it still gives joy to many children in Fantasyland.

As a young boy growing up in Newark in the 1940s, it was only a fifteen-minute bus ride and a short one-block walk to Olympic Park. If my memory serves me correctly, the bus ride was only a nickel and the entrance to the park was about twenty cents. The first place that I normally headed for was my favorite spot — the good old penny arcade.

When the amusement park closed in 1965, what rides had not been sold or moved along with the buildings began to deteriorate and the walkways became overgrown with weeds and shrubs. I'm not certain of the year, but the huge public swimming pool, its shower, and changing rooms became victim to a suspicious fire. Eventually the entire park was cleared and this once great family amusement landmark was replaced with low-income apartments.

My own paranormal experience came forty years later in a dream, the reality of which was so vivid that my belief and the belief of psychic Jane Doherty was that I had actually traveled back to one of the more pleasurable times in my life. Still vivid in my mind, I was standing just outside the open entrance to my favorite spot, the penny arcade, while watching the stroller of my firstborn daughter Karen, who was inside with my wife Ellen. There was a large crowd standing around as well as many passersby. Behind the crowd to my rear, I could see the ring-the-bell tower, where you would hit a seesaw type device with a large wooden mallet that would in turn propel a small metal disk up a cable and hopefully ring the bell at the top.

Before I get to the main part of this experience, I want to fill you in on one piece of information that my wife's mother had passed on back in 1968, may her soul rest in peace, ten years after my wife had given birth to our daughter Karen. As I turned to take a quick look at the crowd standing behind me and hearing the bell being rung several times, I saw my wife's mother walking toward me from out of the crowd. She walked up to me and handed me a few dollar bills saying to use it for the children and then turned, walking back into the crowd and vanishing. This experience has been the only time that my wife's mother has ever appeared to me in a dream.

I am certain that many of us can relate to this type of experience and some not realizing exactly what it is at the time of occurrence. I am also certain that some of Olympic Park's invisible past patrons still return to their old haunt to walk the paths that no longer exist and who may be felt or even seen by residents of the low-income apartment development that still occupies the grounds. Why don't you make a visit there to walk around and speak with some of the residents? One never knows what may be encountered.

EVERGREEN'S NEWSPAPER GHOST

Evergreen Cemetery and Crematory is located on North Broad Street in Hillside and is listed on both the New Jersey Register and

On the sign: **EVERGREEN CEMETERY**

EVERGREEN CEMETERY
ORGANIZED 1853
HAS BEEN PLACED ON THE
NATIONAL REGISTER
OF HISTORIC PLACES
BY THE UNITED STATES
DEPARTMENT OF THE INTERIOR

Above: Entrance to historic Evergreen Cemetery... **Below**: One of the cemetery's two veterans areas... It shows one of the silent sentries guarding the fallen.

the National Register of Historic Places. The cemetery is believed to be one of the largest in the United States and houses many well-known individuals. Its vastness seems never-ending once you begin traveling the winding roads within. You will come across one section that has been specifically set aside for veterans, mostly from the Civil War and wars prior. What is unique about this section is that two, what appear to be, Civil War cannons border the perimeter.

I am including the names of some notable graves simply because of their historical significance. I think you would agree that they could be the reason for the sightings, haunting feelings, and strange changes in atmospheric conditions reported throughout the years here at Evergreen. Interred within are authors Stephen Crane and Edward Stratemeyer; Author Mary Mapes Dodge, best known for her 1865 novel *Hans Brinker or the Silver Skates*; Broadway and Hollywood actor George Houston; and Author Edward Stratemeyer, creator of *The Hardy Boys* (1927) and *Nancy Drew* (1930) book series. The cemetery also is known for having as section of plots devoted to Roma (Gypsy) families.

My personal experience here at Evergreen Cemetery dates back to 1949 after my family had just moved to Hillside from Newark. It all began one summer day just before sunset when my cousin, my friend Bob, and I decided to go for a stroll through Evergreen. Since the cemetery covers quite a large area, it was taking longer than we had thought to complete the rounds of the many roads within. Plus, it was beginning to get dark and it seemed that a summer thunderstorm was beginning to move into the area.

I had stopped for a moment to read one of the interesting inscriptions on a gravestone and, when I began walking again, my cousin and Bob were several yards ahead of me. None of us had watches and I was thinking that if I did not get home soon my parents would have something to say to me. That was when I noticed the figure of a man leaning against a tree reading a newspaper, though it never dawned on me that the light had diminished considerably. The figure, appearing slightly in shadow and wearing a derby hat, seemed a bit intimidating at first, but I decided to approach him to ask the time. Receiving no reply, I asked a second time, but by then my cousin and Bob were quite a distance ahead of

A hidden surprise awaits you at Evergreen...

me. After receiving no reply for the second time, I decided to leave and try to catch up to them; however, after only taking a few steps in their direction, I turned for one last look at the man, mainly to see if he was following me. To my astonishment, he had vanished, but he had left the newspaper that he was reading laying on the ground. I began walking over to pick it up, but before I could reach it...the paper too seemed to simply fade away.

When I told my cousin and Bob what had just happened, they laughed and said that I was seeing things. After a while I began to believe that myself and very rarely told this experience to anyone. Now, not only does it *not* seem so strange, I was also not seeing things. What I experienced that evening in Evergreen Cemetery was a residual haunting.

For both the amateur and more advanced ghost hunter, a word of caution: the gates at Evergreen close at early evening and it would be best to gain permission should you wish to remain after dark.

Chapter Eighteen:

HAUNTED SPRINGFIELD

On June 23, 1780, the climactic battle of the final invasion of New Jersey was fought in Springfield. Approximately 5,000 Crown forces, which included a large contingent of Hessian troops that were under the command of General Knyphausen, attacked from Staten Island, New York, via Elizabethtown, New Jersey, in an attempt to seize the Hobart Gap in the Watchung Mountains and then Morristown. General Greene, with a force of approximately 2,000 Continentals and New Jersey Militia, prevented them from being able to advance to General Washington's Morristown stronghold.

The historic American Revolution Cannonball House...

BATTLE OF SPRINGFIELD
Here, June 23, 1780, 1500 Americans, under Greene and Dayton, were attacked by 5000 British and Hessians under Clinton and Knyphausen enroute to capture stores at Morristown. The British burned Springfield, but were defeated.

This is a side view of the house where cannonballs struck during the Battle of Springfield.

Although the British eventually occupied the town of Springfield, it was not long before they decided to withdraw.

The hard-fought British units were stopped at Springfield through the bravery of Maxwell's Jersey Men, Angell's Rhode Islanders, "Light Horse Harry" Lee's Dragoons, and many others. The town of Springfield was burned to the ground upon the withdrawal of British forces. During the American Revolution, only the British, using it as an act of terror to intimidate the population, burned a handful of towns or communities to the ground. Lexington and Concord were not burned, but Springfield was.

Close-up showing one of the cannonballs and several patched areas where this and others had struck during the battle.

Only four houses survived. Three of them were behind American lines to the South and West and included the historic "Cannonball" House that had been used as a British field hospital and was struck by an American four-pound cannonball during the battle. Today the Cannonball House is owned and run by the Springfield Historical Society. It took fourteen years for the town of Springfield to recover from this battle and to formally incorporate in 1794.

The major thrust of the battle took place along a stretch of the Rahway River that runs through Springfield crossing under Morris Avenue. Large numbers of British soldiers died while attempting to cross this river and many people feel that fact alone lends itself to paranormal activity, which is especially prevalent after a severe thunderstorm. During these storms, the river rises and small artifacts have been discovered washed ashore due to the turbulence stirred up by the water rushing down stream, including uniform belt buckles and buttons, rusted parts of rifles, coins, and musket balls.

I experienced this firsthand while officially photographing historical sites for the Union County Historical Society in the early 1960s. I wanted to take a few photographs in the area of the main battle crossing of the river, but being that it was getting late in the afternoon and I still wanted to photograph the Cannonball House, I only spent a short while there. However, during that time I can recall how still the atmosphere seemed and the odor of gunpowder appeared to permeate the air. After taking a few photographs, I made my way to the Cannonball House. This structure is not very large and upon entering you will immediately be greeted by an unusual feeling...*a feeling that you should not be there*. This is the same feeling that some have in the area of the river.

Now, I cannot recall seeing anything unusual in the photographs that I had taken that day and I believe that they may still be being displayed at the historical society's headquarters. The photographs in this chapter were recently taken as a guide to the locations. There is also a small cemetery that is located near the center of town that you may wish to check out when you visit Springfield — there is an Indian Chief from the battle period resting there.

On a recent visit, the area of the Cannonball House still presents itself in all of its past glory and the nearby branch of the Rahway River still presents a mysterious silence and eeriness.

Part of the historic Rahway River... The King's forces launched their attack on the town of Springfield from here. It now flows, eerily silent, where once was stained with blood.

Chapter Nineteen:

THE SAILOR'S GIRL

KEEPING HER VIGIL

Strange as this may first seem, along a stretch of U.S. Highway 1, just south of the Raritan River Bridge, on a stone mound in the parking lot behind the AMC Loews multiplex, surrounded by a wrought iron fence, you will see the gravesite of the Sailor's Girl. This location was once home to the U.S. Highway 1 Flea Market.

However, it is not what is in the movie theater that is interesting, but what people have seen from time to time *outside* in the parking lot. After all, why would there be a headstone and small graveyard in the parking lot near the river? When I visited here recently, the parking lot behind the theater complex was completely void of automobiles and I could not help but marvel at this huge structure as it came into view. The gravesite was nothing like I remembered from when the flea market occupied this same location. At that time, it was just a simple mound with the wrought iron fence and a headstone.

Back in the days when sailing ships could go up and down Raritan River, Mary Ellis (1750-1827), who was a spinster living in New Brunswick, had fallen in love with a sailor, a sea captain, and it is her grave that now sits rising about six feet above the surface of the parking lot. History allegedly has it that she was seduced by this sea captain who vowed to return to marry her. Unfortunately, Mary waited and waited, but he never did return and it is said that each day Mary would ride her horse to the spot where her grave now stands hoping one day to see his ship sailing up the Raritan and coming home to her.

The song "Brandy" by the New Jersey band Looking Glass is said to have been inspired by the Mary Ellis story. The lyrics include the lines:

"Brandy, you're a fine girl.
What a good wife you would be.
But my life, my lover, my lady is the sea."

The gravesite of Mary Ellis... She is still keeping vigil for her love to return.

Mary's family home eventually became the site for the Route 1 Flea Market and later the Loew's Theater complex. Now just to spice up this story a little, when Mary died, her family, who owned the land, buried her near the river. The family has since sold the land, but always with the caveat that the little grave plot remain. It is rumored that she is buried with her horse that also kept the long lonely vigil with Mary.

Some moviegoers say that they believe Mary's spirit still waits along that section on "The Banks of the Raritan" and that they may have caught a glimpse of her, especially around sunset on the way to their evening's entertainment.

Haunting close-up of the gravestone... It appears to be imprisoned for eternity.

Chapter Twenty:

MILLVILLE ARMY AIR FIELD

SHADOWS OF THE PAST

Stretching a bit further south of Central New Jersey is the sleepy little town of Millville, home to the Millville Airport that was dedicated "America's First Defense Airport" during the Second World War on August 2, 1941. In slightly less than a year, the construction of military base facilities began, and in January 1943, the Millville Army Air Field opened as a gunnery school for fighter pilots.

I have had the opportunity to visit this facility and the museum that is located there many times, as we own property on the outskirts of Millville. Entering the town, while traveling along the main street

This main street is located in the sleepy little town of Millville.

This dedication mural on Main Street greets all of the visitors to Millville.

(High Street), you will experience your first feeling of being taken back to the early 1940s when thousands of military personnel walked these same streets seeking a night's entertainment or simply some relief from the exhaustive daily training at the air field. Towards the end of High Street, looming large, is the municipal complex with the magnificent mural painted on the main building and dedicated to those who served at Millville during the Second World War.

At the base, gunnery training began with the Curtiss P-40F "Warhawk" aircraft, but after a few weeks the P-40s were gone and the Republic P-47 "Thunderbolt" ruled the skies over Cumberland County for the remainder of the war. During its three-year existence, thousands of soldiers and civilians served here with about 1,500 pilots receiving advanced fighter training in the Thunderbolt. Unfortunately some died while training at Millville and this in itself seemingly opens the paranormal door to both interactive and residual hauntings or possibly a combination of both.

The entrance to the Millville Army Air Field Museum...

Sitting silent, the once bustling barracks now houses the spirits of a past conflict.

The Millville Army Air Field Museum (MAAFM) is dedicated to preserving the history of the Millville Army Air Field with its mission to recognize and commemorate all aspects of American aviation history and to document and honor the lives of American veterans, as well as be the proprietor of historic buildings and structures of the World War II period that exist on the site. Still today, many remnants of the airfield's past are being discovered in the fields of the surrounding area, including ordinance from the gunnery training exercises and parts of crashed planes. Many of these and other artifacts, some donated by family members of former pilots who had taken their training here, can be viewed at the museum. When you enter the museum, you will definitely experience the feeling that there may be more to the museum than just the many artifacts on display.

When the Second World War came to an end, so did the Army Air Field — and Millville returned to being a sleepy little town once again. At least once a year my family and I pass through Millville on our way to Cedarville, which is just on the outskirts, to visit a piece of property that has been in the family for many years. On each visit, riding down the main street in Millville, I always get the feeling that some of its past residents, especially those from the World War II period, are still walking the streets and watching from some of the buildings.

Upon first entering the area where the actual base was located, you will come upon the old boarded up cement buildings that once housed the men and other facilities. Only a few are occupied, but most have been deserted. In the distance stands a building that was the old movie theater and one just cannot help but have the feeling that you are traveling into the past. If you listen closely,

One of the displays of World War II military uniforms... an unexpected guardian is captured on film. (Note the energy orb near one of the uniforms.)

Another energy orb acts as the guardian of one the artifacts on display in this showcase.

you can almost hear the roar of the "Thunderbolts" as they take off for their daily training exercises.

In the museum itself many of the artifacts will present a feeling that someone or something is still connected to them — and, in fact, there is! Hanging from a ceiling area is a series of uniforms... among them a silent sentry was captured.

My family and I frequent the area to where our property is located only a couple of miles from the air field and artifacts are still being discovered in the many fields and wooded areas surrounding the airfield. One of my next visits here will be archeological in nature in the hopes of locating some of the artifacts on the property I own.

You won't be remiss for good food should you be traveling along the Atlantic City Expressway in either direction. If you exit at Mays Landing, continuing your journey on Route 40 toward Millville, you will come across the Mays Landing Diner and you will be glad that you stopped.

Chapter Twenty-One:

PROHIBITION SPIRITS UN-BOTTLED

MOB TIES TO NEW JERSEY

Berkeley Township is located in Ocean County and was incorporated by an Act of the New Jersey Legislature on March 31, 1875. It began with Army officer Lt. Edward Farrow, who began buying up woodland with the idea of building a retirement community for former Army and Navy officers. He built a railroad station, shops, and even a resort hotel called "The Pines" in the

Reflected in Crystal Lake is the haunting view of the once, alleged, "mob" hotel.

hopes of attracting people to the area, but only eleven people ever built houses in what Farrow called "Barnegat Park." Eventually, he went bankrupt.

In the 1920s, Benjamin Sangor purchased the area. The New York and Miami developer imagined a vast and luxurious resort town catering to wealthy urban vacationers and, between 1928 and 1929, about 8,000 lots were sold in what was called "Pinewald," a "new type of residential and recreational city-of-the-sea-and-pines." The area was to host a golf course, recreation facilities, and estate homes. The developers immediately began construction of the Pinewald pavilion and pier at the end of Butler Avenue. The Royal Pines Hotel was a $1.175-million dollar investment facing Crystal Lake and was built on the site of an earlier hotel dating back to the days of Barnegat Park. It was the focal point of the new community. The hotel was also used as an asylum and then later as a nursing home. It is now known as the Crystal Lake Nursing & Rehabilitation Center.

Mystery surrounds the former hotel that Russian architect W. Oltar-Jevsky constructed in the early 1920s. Al Capone is said to have frequented its halls and perhaps even venturing beneath the structure to the lake in tunnels that were especially designed for smuggling alcohol during Prohibition. It has been rumored that in the 1930s society's elite frequented the then Royal Pines Hotel and, for $1.90 a drink, consumed prohibition liquor under the watchful eye of men who had guns strapped under their coats. Whether this is fact or merely rumor has since passed into the annals of time.

If you have ever traveled the Garden State Parkway, once you reach the Berkeley Township (Bayville) area, in the distance you will get a glimpse of a large pinkish building that is commonly referred to as Al Capone's Hotel. If you are in the area of Central Regional High School, the structure can easily be seen and is only a stone's throw from there.

As a resident of Berkeley Township, I ventured to this location several times; however, I was never able to gain entrance to investigate. Due to the current use of the building as a nursing home, the owners were reluctant, not wishing the residents to be disturbed or possibly frightened, which is certainly understandable. But just walking the grounds you get an eerie feeling — and can picture in your mind the activity that once had taken place here back in the days of prohibition. Standing on the shoreline of beautiful Crystal Lake, you can picture the many canoes and rowboats with women in long full dresses and holding parasols being paddled by their male escorts in spats and vests, or strolling along the banks of the lake.

If you plan to be there at sunset, I suggest that you ask permission before walking the grounds. I might also suggest that you park your car on the far side of the lake, on the opposite side of the roadway, where you can walk to the lake should you wish to take photographs — you never know what may appear. You may get a glimpse of those bygone days of the mob or overhear a conversation…one that you were not intended to listen to.

Chapter Twenty-Two:

A CAULDRON OF PARANORMAL ACTIVITY

There is a cauldron of paranormal activity within the borders of New Jersey. A person can easily stir up a never-ending flow of spirits and alleged hauntings, as New Jersey is not just known as the Garden State, but is also referred to as the "Most Haunted." Presented here is a listing of some of these alleged haunts for you to consider visiting to satisfy your appetite for the paranormal.

The Woodstown Hotel

An historic and haunted hotel dating from the Revolutionary War period, the Woodstown Hotel has a bar and restaurant. Although this is not the original building, for generations there have been many rumors and stories about this hotel that include George Washington having stayed there, soldier ghosts, mysterious happenings, and even the murder of a child. A ghost with a noose around its neck and other noisy ghosts haunt this place as well.

The owner allegedly refuses to spend the night here and may be eager and willing to have ghost hunters investigate it. Woodstown is a fascinating historical town that has been around since before the Revolutionary War and rumored to be filled with strange auras including the cemetery.

Boonton's Darress Theater

The Darress Theater was closed for many years and was finally bought and used for children's theater while also showing movies there at night. Some people who are there late at night say that they hear voices, footsteps, and that the seats move. There have also been reports of singing coming from the theater when everyone has gone home for the night.

Cape May's World War II Bunker

The magazine at Cape May Point once housed guns to protect the coast from Nazi submarines. A ghostly crew haunts this bunker and spirits of soldiers have also been seen on the beach surrounding it.

Newark's Best Kept Secret

During its heyday, Kresge Department Store was a stop on one of Newark's Subway Lines. Today there is only one line left of the Newark City Subway; all the others, including the one going to Kresge's, are sealed. A New Jersey Transit official made a recent descent down there and the expedition revealed that the storefront Kresge's maintained underground is still intact (except for some broken windows) with mannequins, wooden display cases, and sale signs.

In 1926, the Kresge store at the southwest corner of Broad and Cedar streets arranged to have a platform opened in the subway at its basement level, thereby allowing customers to come in directly from the subway. The station was opened in January 1927 on the inbound side and the only access was through the Kresge store. The old building still stands there as a monument to what it once was during Newark's heyday. The store entrance had large display windows on either side of the doorway leading from the station into the basement, but the transit system's decision to discontinue the Kresge stop prompted the department store to close the basement entrance. Subway cars now could only whiz by on their way to other stops along the route. Eventually the mannequins that had been left on display in the windows became dusty and took on a ghostly appearance...causing some passengers to believe they were seeing ghost-like figures standing on the platform.

Finally, many years later, that section of the subway was closed and blocked off completely, leaving the ghostly mannequins and the deteriorating display windows to history. This changed somewhat, as people were still able to gain entrance to it. As a result, it became a haven for the homeless population. Kresge decided to block the basement entrance completely by sealing it from within.

In my younger years, growing up in Newark, I recall the many visits that my mother and I made to Kresge's, especially at Christmas time to pay my yearly visit to "Good Old Saint Nick." I am not certain as to just what type of business now occupies this location or if the old basement entrance to the subway platform can be located from inside the building; however, if you are bold enough to contact the present occupants or the Newark Transit System to inquire about possible access, this may not be a venture for the faint at heart. But definitely get permission before attempting to enter here. I guess that the inclusion of this bit of history — possibly haunted history — is more along the lines of memory lane while edging on the paranormal. However, it does raise the investigative instinct, doesn't it?

Metuchen — Ayers-Allen House

The Ayers-Allen House is said to be the oldest house in Metuchen and was originally an inn during Revolutionary War times. It's also allegedly haunted by a Revolutionary War soldier, who, at times, is said to have been seen hanging between floors. (Legend has it that he hanged himself.)

Also reported to have been seen at times is the ghost of a woman (the innkeeper's wife) and she is, apparently, still searching for her son who was kidnapped by Indians when he was ten years old. Psychics/mediums have detected the presence of several other spirits that also roam about the house freely, occasionally making their presence known to visitors.

Glendora — Gabriel Davies Tavern

One of New Jersey's oldest historical landmarks, the original furnishings are still in the house that is known as the Gabriel Davies Tavern.

A tavern during the Revolutionary War, the attic was used as a hospital for wounded soldiers — and there are still bloodstains in various parts of the attic, a grim reminder of the many dying and wounded who were brought there. Occasionally sounds have been reported of people walking around upstairs and of individuals in pain, suffering from wounds.

Parsippany — Hilltop Care Center

The Hilltop Care Center is an old abandoned nursing home that at one time had to be evacuated immediately for some unknown reason. All of the patients' files, clothes, pictures — all of their belongings — were left in their old rooms and some may still be found there. When you walk in and out of these rooms, your flashlights will flicker on and off and there is only one door in the whole place that cannot be opened. There is a room reported to be haunted in that when the door was opened, it would stop and then would start to vibrate violently. Presently there is a "NO TRESPASSING" sign posted on the property.

Fort Dix's Haunted Hospital

The hospital at the fort is said to be the home of repeated sightings, noises, and furniture being thrown around on the top five floors. This hospital has seen its share of wartime victims and the basement is where the morgue was located. At times the spirits of some of the hospital's past residents can be seen peering from the windows, presenting visitors with a feeling that there is someone watching you.

Old Tappan

The ghost of a Revolutionary War era bugler for the Continental Army haunts the area around the Old Tappan golf course while other stories say that the sound of a horn (bugle) can be heard in the middle of the night in the wooded area near there. The ghost is simply known as "The Bugler."

Passaic County

On what is now called Annie's Road, a young girl was killed on Prom night (hit by a car) back in the 1980s. It is said that you can see her blood still on the road and at midnight her ghost will come out. Her gravesite is located off of the road where she was killed.

Columbus — The Columbus Inn

The Columbus Inn is a very old restaurant in the center of a very small town where numerous sightings have been alleged throughout the years…even to the extent of having paranormal investigators come in to investigate. This restaurant was featured on television and in the newspapers several years ago. Inside the restaurant, one of the articles can be found behind the bar — it has allegedly been reported that the famous "Jersey Devil" was born here.

Newark's Branch Brook Park

Branch Brook Park is believed to be where a couple who had just gotten married were passing through on the way to their honeymoon when, all of sudden, the groom lost control of his vehicle and crashed into an old tree. The impact was so devastating that the bride was ejected from the car and fell next to the old tree. It is now said that the ground opened and simply swallowed her, but when the police arrived all they found was the groom dead and a piece of white cloth sticking out of the ground. It is believed that she haunts the park at night in her bloody wedding dress. The tree has since been removed, but those living in the neighborhood around the park should be able to direct you to the location where it once stood.

Great Meadow's Ghost Lake

Great Meadow's Ghost Lake was home to American Indians several hundred years ago. Many of them died of malaria and are now said to haunt the area. Many local legends have originated from this area, including one of a "ghostly lake house" that was built in the 1930s and is said to be haunted by former inhabitants who died there. The first individual who built and lived in the house went crazy and killed his wife and daughter, whose bodies are supposedly buried on the property.

Frenchtown

At first glance, Frenchtown appears to be what you would term as "Any-Town USA" during the daytime, but as the darkness of the night falls, the phantoms of bygone days in this town appear, apparently wishing not to move on. Many of the locals will tell you that there are no spirits, but if you are fearless enough to spend the night in Frenchtown…you may spot just a spirit for yourself.

Frenchtown is the site of the now shuttered National Hotel that has played a significant role in the history of this area. During the 1930s, poet, novelist, and screenwriter James Agee lived on the street behind the National. Apparently he found the environs of the hotel well-suited to his lifestyle and his talent — much of his work from that period was accomplished while sitting at the bar.

During the late 1800s, the famous Annie Oakley would visit Frenchtown with her fellow performers from Bill Cody's Wild West Show. When in town, the National was always their preferred watering hole.

Cranford — Gallows Hill Road

Located at the corner of Gallows Hill Road and Brookside Place stood a huge tree from which spies were hanged during the Revolutionary War. The tree was cut down a few years ago, but the rusty iron and concrete post to which the hangman's rope was tied still stands.

Howell/Allaire — Allaire Village

Historic Allaire Village is located in the middle of the park on Allaire Road where reports of a female apparition in white has been spotted between the park and the General Store. However, what is interesting about the village is the presence of significant quantities of bog iron ore. This bog ore was so called because of its formation in marshes and swampy areas and was a valuable resource in America before the discovery of vast ore deposits in the mountains of Northern New Jersey and Pennsylvania. Unlike the latter ore, though, bog ore is easily accessible and requires no deep shaft of strip mining to get it. Where there is iron, there is rust — and that lends itself to recording residual hauntings. As a result, should you wish to pay a visit to this historic site, you will see people walking around in period clothes and, while some of them may be reenactment actors... *others may not be.*

Ringwood — Ringwood Manor Cemetery

Shadows may be seen and voices heard in this more than century-old family cemetery. The aboveground tombs have bricks that are continually missing or chipped away and evidence shows that this action is coming from *within* the tomb rather than by outside vandalism. As you walk through the "Gates to Nowhere" and follow the path along the pond, the cemetery will begin on your left and continue in spots for approximately half a mile.

Toms River — Castle Park

At Castle Park, an unusual phenomena is said to take place at midnight — all the swings begin to sway in rhythm at the same time without any sign of wind being present. Some have claimed to hear the sound of children playing when no one is around. Castle Park is located near the Dover Township Police complex by the Bay Lea Golf Course. Should you plan on being here at midnight some dark moonlit night, I would suggest letting the police know why and what you will be doing there.

Castle Park is allegedly haunted. *Courtesy of NJGO member Cathy Sansevere.*

Ancora — Veterans Haven

The Veterans Haven's location is right next to the Bayside Prison and Ancora Mental Institution. It was once a town the psychiatric hospital made for patients to all live together and it was there that many of the patients murdered each other, most of whom were old veterans. Eventually there were so many killings, the whole town was simply shut down. There is still a great deal of paranormal activity and, unusual as it may seem, the streetlights are still left on throughout this little known deserted ghost town.

Historic Hightstown

Located in Central New Jersey is a sleepy little town that is split by U.S. Highway 33 and was established in 1721. When you visit here, you will certainly not run out of excellent places to eat; however, you may be sharing a table or a bench in the park with one of the long past residents of this little borough...*a spirit of yesteryear*.

New Brunswick — Rutgers University

Who would ever imagine that ghosts would wander about an institute of learning? Well, they do at Rutgers University. It is not really surprising though when you consider that the main campus at New Brunswick, a land-grant and state supported co-educational university (except for Douglass College), was chartered in 1766 as Queen's College and opened its doors in 1771.

At the beginning of the Revolutionary War, Rutgers (then known as Queen's College) was in its infancy. With the occupation of New Brunswick by the British at the time of the war, Queen's College carried on its work at other locations. Many of the students and faculty became involved in the American Revolution, most of whom became known for their activities at the federal and local government level. Others were chiefly noted for their patriotic activity. Noted students include Simeon Dewitt, class of 1776, who became the Surveyor General of the United States and mapped areas for George Washington during the war, and James Schureman, class of 1775, fought beside John Taylor, an early tutor of the college, and later became a member of the U.S. Congress. Many of the early students either became involved in politics and law or became preachers.

So it's not too hard to believe then that as Rutgers — and New Brunswick — grew...*so did its specter population*.

Metlar-Bodine House

The historic Metlar-Bodine House located in Piscataway was built in 1728 by Peter Bodine and is the older of two remaining buildings from the colonial port of Raritan Landing. Entrepreneur George Metlar, wishing to make the house his residence, purchased the home and property. Many of the historic artifacts and documents of the period are on display in the house, including a wall that was saved from Ross Hall — where allegedly George Washington celebrated Independence Day back in 1778. The wall is one of the home's major attractions. Records have it that from July 1st to the 7th of that same year Gen. Washington and approximately 11,000 Continental soldiers set up camp on the banks of Raritan River. Even though Ross Hall no longer stands, the remnants of that period have been well preserved at the Metlar House.

Renowned Psychic Jane Doherty paid a visit to the Metlar-Bodine House to investigate the reported paranormal activity. Immediately Jane felt the presence of many spirits in the house, including those with a connection to the famous Hall-Mills murder trial *(see Chapter 12)*. Jane also was able to detect a presence that was in close proximity to the robe of the judge who had presided over this trial. The presence of spirits was also detected near other exhibits.

In 2003, a considerable number of the artifacts became victim to a fire, but fortunately the structure itself and the contents from many of the rooms were able to be saved. Tragic as this was, it has not seemed to deter the spirit activity in the home.

Livingston Barracks

The Livingston Barracks are an interesting slice of history located on the Piscataway side of the Old Raritan (Raritan River). The barracks were constructed in the 1940s and were former military housing actively used by the Camp Kilmer Station until Rutgers University acquired all of the 122 structures in 1963. The ghostly long gray buildings are located at the furthest west end of the

Livingston campus and it is alleged that at one time these buildings held Prisoners of War and served as a wartime station, complete with a hospital and prison. As you give some thought to those sixty years ago — where people today sit at their desks in the building on street number 1604, Prisoners of War bided their time until they could once again be united with their families — undeniable is the unrest and dark history that may have surrounded this place in times past.

Merriwood Castle

As difficult as it may seem to believe, there is a castle in nearby Highland Park sitting, just off of River Road and across the street from Johnson Park, in all of its Medieval splendor. The stones that were used to build the castle block by block were imported from the Cotswold area of England more than seventy-five years ago. Believed to have twenty-five rooms, the castle is complete with hidden stairwells and secret passageways. Originally the owners of the castle were John Seward Johnson, who was heir to the Johnson and Johnson fortune, and his wife Ruth Dill. After their divorce, Ruth married Phillip Crockett in 1940 and they moved into the carriage house. From 1947 to 1963, the castle was the residence of Charles and Barbara Farmer and their children. For part of this time, it also served as a nursing home. This now becomes interesting as Charles Farmer was charged in the shooting death of his estranged wife in 1963 as she stopped by to pick up some of her belongings. Charles entered the bedroom through a secret passageway and snuck up on his wife, shooting her three times. Charles then shot himself, but the wounds weren't fatal and he was admitted into a mental institution. The Castle was uninhabited for five years after the murder, but is now home to realty offices.

Chapter Twenty-Three:

THE TIME WARP CONTINUUM

Continuum (theory) is anything that goes through a gradual transition from one condition to a different condition without any abrupt changes. The terms — *time warp, space warp,* and *time-space warp* — often reference Einstein's theory that time and space form a continuum that bends, folds, or warps from the observer's point of view, relative to such factors as movement or gravitation. However, they are also used in reference to more fantastic notions of discontinuity or other irregularities in space-time not based on real-world science.

Let me begin by first stating a scientific fact that matter, as we know it, cannot be created or destroyed, but from a paranormal perspective it can be left behind, thereby explaining certain paranormal occurrences. Before getting into what constitutes a true time warp, to those who may be familiar with spirits and ghosts and how they are connected and to the readers who may not be, it is paramount to absorb fully the experiences in the sections that follow to have a better understanding of what they some day may encounter.

As explained in Chapter One, in the paranormal community, there are two kinds of hauntings: one is what we refer to as being a human spirit that is interactive, the second being residual or "ghosts." The latter is the one that we will be concerned with when discussing time warps. A residual haunting is considered the most common by paranormal researchers, as the extreme energy emitted at the time of a traumatic occurrence or in any situation can be recorded in the environment. When you experience the sound of phantom footsteps, images, apparitions, or scents, these may be part of a recorded playback (residual haunting). There is no interaction with the living — *the ghost does not see or hear you* — because it is not actually there. Only their energy remains…it is a remnant of their living form that you are seeing. This cycle continues in the same place at usually the same time of day or year indefinitely, either until the energy is exhausted or diminishes to a low enough level that it is undetectable by human perception.

Residual hauntings occur when the surrounding conditions are right and when what is known as the "veil" thins, presenting itself as a scene of an event that may have taken place in a different time period and that will replay itself over and over, very similar to that of a looped videotape. This scene was somehow recorded in time, in the atmosphere of the surroundings, near or where it had once taken place. When I stated "the veil thins," paranormal phenomena will take place more often and more easily when the atmospheric conditions are similar to those created when there is thunderstorm activity in the air.

Exactly what is the connection between a residual haunting and a time warp? The answer to this is simple as most paranormal researchers consider them to be one-in-the-same. For instance, you may be walking in an area and, as you turn a corner, suddenly you find yourself in the position of seeing or being in an unfamiliar setting...a time warp! I do not want you to confuse these thoughts with time travel, as it is not the same thing — you *cannot* interact with any of the actors in the scene or with any part of the scene itself. Now, this may be oversimplifying it a bit, but as we delve into this subject more deeply I am certain that you will gain a clearer understanding, as there are other factors that may have a direct connection or have an affect consummating a time warp.

Although close in structure, the major differences that distinguish the residual haunting from a true time warp are several in nature. Being the most common are visual images of human form appearing in a repetitive pattern or that of hearing voices, a conversation, and possibly seeing an apparition around the same time of day and when no one else is around. A true time warp contains similar factors, but with the one exception being that you can unknowingly become an invisible part of it and at times not even realize it. When this situation should occur, there are telltale signs that will help you to realize this: 1. You cannot physically touch any item within the scene; 2. You should be able to easily pass through objects, including human images in the scene, almost as if you were a spirit yourself; and 3. You are unable to communicate verbally with the scene's ghostly participants. In my opinion, you have absolutely nothing to fear except for having the initial human reaction of wonder in not knowing exactly what is transpiring.

"Time Warps" reveal the ghostly treasures of past happenings that have left their imprint in time — a paranormal history. From the beginning of time here on earth as we know it, human existence has created circumstances, both pleasurable and traumatic that are relived over and over when the conditions are right. The terms given to this phenomenon are "residual" or "residual haunting" and are often compared to the data stored on a video recorder.

Time warps or time tears have been experienced by living humans throughout the ages and are not inherent to any one location. Anyone can experience one at any given time or place when the conditions are right. Being a paranormal phenomenon, it will be a dimensional experience that will not soon be forgotten. The naysayer will always be skeptical until such time as they have experienced this phenomenon.

I have always given thought as to what the outcome would be should two living humans enter the same time warp from opposite directions or together from the same direction: would they be able to interact with each other? Due to one of my personal experiences, which you'll read about later in this chapter, I believe that it is more probable than just a possibility, as I had interaction with my family while never leaving the confines of our automobile and creating what may be a unique situation...that of remaining within our time period while inside the environment of a time warp. A bubble within a bubble!

With his permission, the following excerpt is quoted from Paul Kimball, a Paranormal TV Host and Investigator:

"Could ghosts be time travelers? Assume for the moment that ghosts are real in the sense that they represent an anomalous, paranormal phenomenon (or at least some of them do). As with UFOs, that begs the question: what are they?

Again, as with UFOs, there may well be a myriad answers. The one that most people latch onto right off the bat is that ghosts are the spirits of deceased people who remain in touch, somehow, with our plane of existence. The other popular answer that I hear most often is that what we think of as ghosts are, in at least some cases, demons of some sort.

Perhaps, but what if ghosts are something else? Could it be possible that what we see or experience as a ghost represents a break in the continuum of time? In other words, if we view time as not a linear construct, but rather a wave, or even a loop, could we be looking backwards (or perhaps even forwards) in time when we observe a ghost, or similar phenomena? The person we see or experience, assuming that they are from the past, is in all likelihood dead (although if it's the recent past, they may well still be alive in our time), but as we observe them, it is as if through a portal, fleeting though it may be, to the past. In short, they are still alive when we are looking at them, at least in their time.

This strikes me as just as plausible an answer for ghosts than the "spirits of the dead" idea (although the two are not necessarily mutually exclusive). Religious scholars have always spoken about some manifestation of an "eternal now." Scientists now openly speculate that human-initiated time travel in some form or another might be possible. But what if the "time travel" is occurring naturally, as opposed to the human-created forms we usually dream about?

Maybe, just maybe, when we see a manifestation of someone dressed as if they were in the 1890s, they really are still in the 1890s...even as they are, for a moment in time, also in 2009."

THE TOWN THAT VANISHED

My first experience with a time warp or, to be more precise, a time tear, takes me back to the summer months of the 1970s. My wife and I, with our four children, were returning from a weekend of camping at a site we had purchased a year or so earlier; one where we could leave our camper year-round in the northeastern part of Pennsylvania, not too far over the New Jersey border.

Deciding to take a different route home instead of driving back down the New Jersey side of the Delaware River, we drove south down Route 611 on the Pennsylvania side, crossing over into Frenchtown, New Jersey. Usually on our way home from camping my wife liked to stop along the route to pick up fresh fruit and vegetables and most of the time we had no difficulty in locating a roadside stand. This time, though, was the exception, as it was not until we had crossed back into New Jersey that we were able to locate one. After traveling a few miles, we spotted a small sign by the side of the road that read "fresh fruit and vegetables" with an arrow pointing down a narrow dirt road. I mentioned to my wife that we had better not take too much time as the sun had just set and it was beginning to look and feel as though we were going to have some thunderstorm activity. Thinking that we would only have to go a short way, we began what was to become an unexpected journey into the past.

After traveling for about a quarter of a mile and seeing no stand, I said to my wife that we had better forget about looking for the stand and find a place to turn around and continue heading for home, as the sky was looking even more like a thunderstorm was brewing. No sooner did I finish talking, I could see in front of me a round type structure, which resembled a gazebo of sorts — the kind you would see in a town square. As we slowly approached, we could see that the road separated and you could go either to the left or to the right, forming a circle with the gazebo in the center.

The roadway around the circle was lined with several Victorian style houses, old and seemingly in dire need of paint. This little town circle appeared a bit strange as it seemed to be void of any human life — someone should have been around yet there was no one. Everything was shrouded in an eerie silence like a veil of death had just dropped from nowhere.

I stopped the car for a moment and was about to get out to go to one of the houses to ask about the stand when my wife grabbed my arm and told me to forget about it. She was concerned about getting the children home before we got caught in severe thunderstorms. I noticed that the air had become still and the sky was taking on an eerie yellowish hue and I do not know if it was my "sixth sense" kicking in, but something told me to turn the car around and get out of there as fast as I could!

When we returned home, my wife and I simply could not erase from our minds the unusual experience that we had, so a few weeks later, leaving the children at home this time, we decided to return to the scene of the crime. We located the dirt road, but noticed something strange — the old sign advertising fresh fruit and vegetables was no longer there. However, we decided to travel in anyway. This time upon reaching the old town circle there was no gazebo and no houses dotting its perimeter. The circular roadway was overgrown with weeds and bushes… All trace of what we had seen a couple of weeks earlier simply seemed to have completely disappeared!

After this second experience, it was the topic of discussion for a short while, but was soon tucked away in our minds; at least until I became interested in the paranormal when, once again, it became a prime topic. The only difference between the time of occurrence and now was that thirty some years had passed. Discussing it now makes more sense to me as to what had actually occurred on that day back in the 1970s. I feel that we had the rare privilege of being exposed to a wonderful phenomenon, that of a time warp — a tear in the fabric of time — in which we took a momentary trip into history

TO "BEE" OR NOT TO BE

It was early July 2008 and we were in Long Beach, California, visiting my wife's brother Steve. Fourteen years earlier was the last time we had Steve, who was ninety-four and living in a small ranch house. On this visit, our youngest son accompanied us on the long flight out. The flight was a pleasant one, but we had no idea as to what lay ahead of us on a surprise visit to the *H.M.S. Queen Mary*.

Built during the Jazz era of the 1930s, the luxury passenger liner was converted for use as a troop carrier during the Second World War and was dubbed "The Gray Ghost," deriving its nickname from having been repainted battleship gray so that it could blend into the horizon and, therefore, be hidden easily from enemy vessels. After the war, the *Queen Mary* reverted to its original use as a luxury passenger ship. Now retired and berthed permanently in the harbor at Long Beach, the *Queen Mary* was converted into a hotel. However, the ship has not lost the charm of the 1930s when it was used as a luxury liner.

This ship has a history of being extremely haunted and paranormal tours for the public are conducted daily and on weekends. During World War II, on October 2, 1942, the *Queen Mary* collided with its escort ship, the British Light Cruiser *Curacoa*, cutting it in half and damaging a section of her bow, which allowed the sea to rush in and resulted in the sudden and untimely death of over three hundred men within minutes. Many of the bodies were found in this bow section due to the suction created by the seawater rushing in.

Little did we know when we arrived at Steve's home that he had a surprise in store for us — the next day he was taking us to visit the *Queen Mary* as it was a special day for him. The ship was being closed to the general public in honor of veterans, firemen, police, and their families who would be able to visit the ship free that day. Steve, being a thirty-year veteran of the United States Navy and of the Second World War, was looking forward to us coming along with him. Having just heard stories and seeing photographs of this sea-going city, one could never imagine the true magnificence of this Queen of the Sea until you actually set foot upon her decks. Visiting the ship's inner beauty was truly like taking a step back in time.

A few months before leaving on our trip, I had purchased a new video camcorder, the kind that used the new disk instead of the 8mm tapes, and was anxious to bring it along to California. I had checked it out to make sure it was in fine working order just prior to our trip.

The first area of the ship that we visited was the upper deck at the bow where a reminder of World War II still stood in the form of one of the four anti-aircraft that once protected the troop ship from enemy attack. The other three have since been removed, passing into history. After standing at the bow for several minutes, taking in the beautiful surrounding scenery, my wife and son began to walk toward the area where the gun emplacement was. As they approached the few steps leading down to it, I began videotaping as I followed them. Everything seemed normal until, out of nowhere, a huge swarm of bees came buzzing around us. Keeping my camcorder running, I began to motion my free arm in an attempt to push the bees away from me, but to my astonishment, as thick and as many as there were, I could not make contact with them… but I could *hear* them buzzing loudly. My wife and son seemed to be calling to me, but I could not hear them — I could only hear the buzzing of the bees swarming around me. Finally, as quickly as they appeared, they were gone. Once I had caught up to where my son and wife were standing, they asked me why did I not stop recording and move more quickly, as they were yelling and motioning to me to move faster. I told them that I didn't hear anything but the buzzing of the bees, adding that their motions seemed to be in a sort of slow motion. My wife and son had experienced the beginning of this phenomena as they were slightly ahead of me.

Later during the visit I discussed the incident with several of the ship's crewmembers. I wanted to inform them of what had happened so that they may possibly search for a hive somewhere in that area. I was told that this has happened on several occasions, as other visitors have also reported it, but when searched there was no hive to be found at, near, or at any other location on the ship. They added that it has been accepted as being a definite part of the haunting taking place on and inside the ship.

It was truly fortunate that I had kept my camcorder running at the time as the experience was documented. When played back, you can see and hear the bees. You almost get the feeling that you can touch them, but we know now that they weren't "touchable," as they did not really exist in our time. Rather, they were a remnant of a past time, a scene being replayed at various times when the conditions are right — it was an experience that none of us there that day will ever forget and one that has been preserved for others to share.

LOST iN TiME

Devil's Den is considered to be a hotspot for paranormal activity at Gettysburg, Pennsylvania and has not changed much in the 144 years since the battle was fought, which could account partially for the high level of paranormal activity that takes place there. For the spirits that exist in this location, the surroundings look exactly as they did the day that they died, a factor that could lead the restless ghosts to believe that the war has never ended and why they continue to fight the same battle day after day. Residual hauntings have been reported as being a common occurrence at the Civil War's Gettysburg Battlefield and I am certain that many of these have actually been time warps, as I reconstruct one such instance that took place there.

On a visit to the Civil War battlefield, Maryanne Vasnelis, a psychic with the New Jersey Ghost Organization, unknowingly, was about to experience the unusual. Though she was hoping to encounter some paranormal activity, Maryanne was not totally prepared for what was about to happen.

Being a psychic, Maryanne is not shaken easily, but on this particular day, beginning as any normal visit would to this historic battlefield, things changed drastically for Maryanne and her friends. The sun was setting and Maryanne's friends were already heading down from the huge rock formation to the parking lot below. However, Maryanne had lagged behind, causing her friends to become worried that something had happened to her. Waiting a bit longer, they called up to her and, receiving no reply, they continued calling her name…with still no response. Maryanne should have easily heard them calling, but for some apparent reason, unbeknownst to them, she could not! Strange as it may seem, Maryanne was calling out to them, but they also could not hear her.

By now, as their calling turned to shouting, her friends were becoming frantic, but finally relief came as Maryanne appeared, still not knowing why she could not hear them calling to her. As she approached them, they asked what had happened that she did not respond to their frantic calls to her. At first, the simple answer that Maryanne gave was that she didn't hear anyone calling. But as it turns out Maryanne had encountered something unusual — a tear in the fabric of time or a time warp. It was something that she had only heard of prior to this experience. Now, I will let Maryanne relate what she actually experienced in her own words.

"I felt as if something was holding me back as I attempted to descend the steps leading to the path to the parking area. When I finally was able to continue and met up with my friends who were waiting for me at the head of the path, I, as well as they, breathed a sigh of relief. Asking me where I had been and why I had not returned their shouts to me, I told them that I did not hear them calling and asked them, 'Didn't you hear me?' They answered, 'No, but others were coming down the path from the rock formation and you would have seen them.' I saw no one — all was quiet and the air was still and a heavy feeling came over me. Anyone coming down would have had to pass by me and no one did. All in all twenty minutes had passed since they began calling to me…twenty lost minutes that cannot be accounted for, but to me it only seemed like a few. During this time I did not experience any spirit presences…just the feeling of being held back. After this experience, I realized that I had been privileged to have been in a time period other than my present one."

After hearing about Maryanne's encounter, I am of the firm belief that this may not have been the first time that a visitor to Gettysburg has experienced a similar phenomenon. This may be especially true during the time that the reenactment of the battle takes place…as that activity may stir up the atmosphere creating a thinner veil and promoting spirit activity. But wait — it doesn't end here. Maryanne relayed an incident experienced by another individual on one of her visits, which occurred during a battle reenactment. While speaking with one of the reenactors who was portraying a period soldier, they passed on the following story to her…

He was with a friend who was also portraying a soldier; however, they became separated and when they finally reunited again, his friend seemed to be a bit disoriented and dazed. All that he could recall was that he saw a general on horseback and was ordered to join the other troops. He could recall absolutely nothing after that experience and was told that several hours had passed since they had become separated.

Could the friend have seen a "ghost" general on horseback giving an order to another spirit soldier who may have been standing in close proximity to the reenactor and not speaking directly to him? Caught in a time warp would be a more plausible explanation.

EPILOGUE

If certain theories are to be believed, then hauntings are caused by high emotions, trauma, and pain that leave scars on buildings and objects. It stands to reason, therefore, that certain structures simply lend themselves to such markings. Filled to the brim with refuse and memories, what happens to those places when society no longer has use for them? They stand empty, keeping their secrets and simply providing a home for restless souls for all of eternity; souls that wait in the hopes that one day someone, anyone, will come inside to glimpse the past and make contact with them. As paranormal investigators, this may by our destiny, and those with the psychic gift, to free these souls, helping them to move on.

I have only been able crack open the paranormal door of what awaits you here in New Jersey in areas where I have had personal experiences or have heard instances over the years and featuring some of the New Jersey Ghost Organization's major investigations. The remainder will be yours, my dear readers, to discover and experience.

It would be remiss of me not to stress that some of these locations may be currently off limits to public access and that it would be wise to either check with the owner or in some cases the authorities before attempting to enter. I know that NJGO has made it their practice to get permission whenever possible.

To all of my readers, I certainly hope that you enjoyed reading about some of the haunted locations here in Central New Jersey and that you have gained an insight into "Ghost Hunting." I wish you all the best of luck with your quest into the world of the paranormal….

INDEX